Contents

Vol 94 No 2 Summer 2004

Poems

Essays

Reviews

Poet in the Gallery

Art

Poems

Andrew Waterman

MR CARNIVAL BOUNCES BACK

Now they are at it in broad daylight:
with pastepot and brush where an alley dips to the Corso
the beaming features of Burro, Doddo, Pino,
Carnevale, Cincotta, Marmora, Nano,
are effaced by the smile and slogan of Bartolo Ziino.
The activists nod at their work, scamper off.
Candidate Carnevale will bounce back.

It is the election for the Provincial Council
of Messina, whereunder fall the Aeolian Islands.
And there are so many parties, their posters plastered
in Lipari town on all possible walls,
around the island, at Lami, at Quattropani,
and the other islands. On churches, on wayside waste-bins.
The conflict seesaws: up or down
each morning are Doddo, Nano, Burro, Ziino,
Chiara Giorgianni (the only woman) and Pino.
Avvocato Carnevale always bounces back.

Another night's work, again his thick lips
in a clean sweep: three rows of twelve of him
at via Roma, via Franza, Marina Corta.
Vulnerable, true, to his rivals' pastepot hirelings –
but can they pay for so many posters?
Marmora, Pino, Cincotta, Burro, Ziino,
have bit-parts merely in these mural medleys.

Of course, there are business interests. 'No, not mafia,
not exactly,' Marisa tells me,
'but men with influence. Votes buy favours.'
At the south tip of the island, from the wall
of the Observatory (a converted watchtower)
Mr Carnival (times twenty) scans the cosmos.

I am told anecdotes about Carnevale,
his legendary wealth and his gluttony.
He was a young *avvocato* when, in the 'sixties,
tourists first came, to save the islands' economy.
The grateful *liproti* decided to feast them.
'Do not', counselled Carnevale, 'ply them with octopus,
swordfish, squid. Offer them something exotic.
Gateau!' He had to explain:
'No, not *gatto*', cat, 'but a rich French *torta*.'
So they bought many kilos of potatoes
in order to make more *gateau*, and more cheaply,
rigged up a hall with bunting and coloured streamers,
and invited the tourists. Who, when at last
the potato-gateau was cooked, got scarcely a morsel:
Mr Carnival was wolfing the lot.
So the local youth, to chastise his discourtesy,
took down paper streamers, stuffed them under
his chair, and ignited them: whoosh!
But Mr Carnival bounced back.

'His family', Guy tells me, 'had a car
when most of us still rode donkeys. They would remove
each summer for the three hottest months,
as the smart set did, to the heights of Pianoconte,
five kilometres above the town.
Then he inherited land in Calabria.
He came back on the *nave* with a battered suitcase
crammed with 500,000-*lire* notes.
A strange way for a lawyer to transfer a fortune.'

Carnevale's party, Alleanza Nazionale,
are *alla destra*, but no, they are not fascists –
fascist parties are not legal in Italy.
Gli eoliani votano un eoliano
reads his poster-slogan. 'That is,' says Guy,
'"Donkeys vote for a donkey".'

Now Mr Carnival plans a further party.
Vi invito, a poster in shops (including Guy's:
'I am a democrat, it is free speech'),
I invite you to Piazza San Cristofero
at Canneto for an evening of music, dancing,
and refreshments. Avv. Carnevale.
England has not seen the like since, in *Pickwick Papers,*
Dickens wrote-up the Eatanswill election.

A sweep round the bay from Marina Lunga, the tunnel
cut through the great lava promontory, a twirl
of road, and here is the *lungomare*
of Canneto, under a gibbous moon.
And there is such scoffing and quaffing, yes, I partake,
and a girl in jeans performs cartwheels around the piazza,
while another, backed by guitars, sings *Il ballo twist*:
Let's-a tweest again like-a we deed last summer,
Let's-a tweest again like-a we deed last-a year . . .
Mr Carnival rises to speak,
wearing a suit and tie, flashing his teeth . . .
But God, perhaps, is not an Aeolian
or, if he is, votes Doddo or Nano or Pino.
The heavens open: a downpour, thunder, lightning.
We are all put to flight.

Undeterred, Mr Carnival bounces back:
Vi invito etc, now to Marina Corta,
where he has commandeered the Café du Port.
And when, after feasting and music and dancing,
he rises to speak, it seems that God has relented,
we listen under tranquil night sky.
'I promise you nothing' (orotund tones, florid gestures)
'that I will not deliver. For the young,
campi sportivi . . . And, for the old' – this and that.
'For our fishermen – seas full of fish.' Next, Education.
Aeolians must be graduates! For Canneto
a university . . . For Acquacalda
an airport. And for the donkeys of Alicudi,
autostrade . . .' I look up,
and the Man in the Moon winks back.

Carnevale is elected.
'We *liparoti*', Guy's arms fling out,
return to roost on his brow, 'are *idioti*!
What were we doing when the rest of Italy
had the Renaissance, da Vinci, Raffaello,
Tiziano, Michaelangelo?
I will tell you – being beaten up by the Turks
and dragged away in their ships into slavery!'
He glances across the Corso: 'Avvocato!
Avvocato Carnevale, *venga qua!*'
The politician bobs across
from the thronging *passegiata*, clad now in shorts
and vivid open-neck shirt, is bronzed from the sun.
Guy introduces me in rapid Italian
as 'your greatest admirer, at all your meetings,
who only laments that his vote is confined to England . . .'
 Mr Carnival flashes his teeth, pumps my arm –
and before I get back a word rejoins his companions,
bouncing away like a beachball along the Corso.

UNITED ITALY

Traffic-lights, they say, in Milan give instructions,
in Rome they offer suggestions, in Naples they are
Christmas decorations. Here in the seven
Aeolian Islands there are no traffic-lights.

All flows, cutting corners, vrooming up alleys behind one,
passing wrong-side, threading strollers along the Corso
('closed' to vehicles at six; but where are the *carabinieri*?).
They are artists at last-second jinking to miss each other,

and you and me. Rosa lives in the narrowest *vicolo*
in town, her drying-rack leaves no way for the dinkiest
motorino; yet when she returns from work at the butcher's
(or sometimes the baker's, but now again at the butcher's)

the contraption's intact; and no-one has stolen her knickers.
While up in Milan among gridlock and raging policemen
the *babygangster* swarm out of school to start mugging:
cellphones, designer clothes, keeping up with their peer-group.

Shirtless, pouring more wine (his children cavorting
outside where mountain shoulders the stars, and I wonder
how ever they get up for school), 'Never', says Enzo,
'was Italy unified! 1861 was a Savoyard

putsch! Restore us our Bourbons!' (Northerners jested
that Sicily joining was less any unification
of Italy than the division of Africa.)
An ironist, Enzo may not mean his last sentence.

Daljit Nagra

THE EVENTUAL COMING OF THE COLOURED PEOPLE . . .

From being the clean-cut with straight A's, I flipped,
went left, snarling as a punk through an out-of-bounds
corridor where the ceiling hailed me with enthusiasms
of wet paint fobbed on the moons of my fingers,
against my uniform dun tenor the coronation songed
whispering kaleidoscopes of wodge mixer worlds.

I watched it cake, and candle for a jubilee of days,
my mother went red cussing me *gunda*, blinding
me all over with a halo-light of her black-and-white scrub;
rust-blanched until an inscape of trumpet-grunged chaos
blew me out from the fortress of her home. Un-noosing my tie,
I ran for the sublime dabbling of my dumbed mind.

Spitting prissy vocab at the blue, ragging and rolling
my palimpsest limbs, I raved bang off date,
lunched on the jam of vowels from mango or indigo
tongues, tilted an ear for the word made fresh
at the markets of subliminal-pink and scuzzy verbs
where they put a cappella to the bromium gobs of gutters.

I stopped out with a lingua franca of waywards,
we felt wronged by ordered code of rainbow
and went in search for the womb of a flamey fleck-planet,
for the *om* of its molten mandala that would splurge
the words and colours of the world through our gaping skin
so our skin and seeing were a carnival-weave of its

aurora aura.

ALL WE SMILEY BLACKS

The orient sun has zapped away the sepia,
floating our revamped brownfield with a serenade
of warmth. The Parky hollers, *comin queekly heeya*
dis da neww parrrrk! With a switch he bouquets
rockets of confetti flowering on our regiments of speakers,
tricksters, clowns, crowds, drummers and songsters,
all of us marching for the entrance in our native gears.

Bullets of light glow-up the applauding leaves
and bolt through the petticoat parade of saplings
as the grass lets go with a to-and-fro of Mexican waves
for masked children who kick from orange swings,
some dive in the spongy sand-pit for hide and seek,
as we improvise with a massive khaki ground-sheet
feasting on our picnic of chapattis and patties and teas.

A humble-looking man receives a grenade shaped chum-chum
with its leaking syrup from a low-caste smiling woman,
another drowns his lover with almondy puffs
through dandelion clocks that fluff her thread of buttons.
The Parky chants with his totem-wand at the heavens,
summoning clouds that outline nations of the globe,
his wand now merges the map! World in a soft

pink bulge of mingling mass on our patch of Slough.
One drops her juggling skittles for their oceanless
borderless; she is ear to ear, on her knees, with bouts
of laughter as she imagines jogging to her father's in Africa.
Another swarthy person points: *is that cloud for India*
and England? Is this Magic or Maya? Are we freed
from Shiva, in our settling, as we dance for Brahma?

A PRELUDE TO SUKA'S ADVENTURES FROM THE BOARD ROOM

He was the first from our farms on a cheap boat ride to Britain;
       within a year of work, showered
with overtime, he sent home his pounds for an Enfield bike.
       Dripping in black and silver
it posed in the courtyard. Our scooters farting on the parched
       soil as we left-behinds would meet
to be drawn by the pull from the flood of his letters that swore
       on swift returns for a small price.

I crossed the sea, like those Englishmen who made their names abroad,
       for his damp and graffiti'd house
where he threw up a panel of chip wood on the bath, and titled
       this my bedroom. Whispering
there's a stream of shift-working men, sleeping days or nights,
       swamping the shared space.
Then he sucked the chain on his steaming piss. In the kitchen
       he fed me cardboard chappatis.

I had left my wife, and the drip of mail from wherever
       at my village postal job,
for this once always-drunk, street-sweeper's boy made good.
       When I asked about the button
pushing work he'd gushingly written of, I almost choked
       at his head on a body of stick,
at the ash of ghostly hair and the sunken eyes
       as he laughed and laughed through his yellow teeth.

Lucie McKee

THANKSGIVING

Snug house in the snow troubled by the mute makers of
everything here. Roof. Walls. Stove. Exhaust fan.
Drain board. Stair. Water flowing hot and cold. Working
furnace. Hands everywhere, and from the kitchen
sink a belly laugh. Drawings on the fridge by U.S. kids.
Shelved authors their spines impressed by publishers.
Hard drive and software – Big shots and thousands of
Doe's – lone makers of twenty-two million bytes.
The music totem pole of: speakers>CDs>producers>
composers. Each name, please, in lights. A rug
woven by Egyptian kids. My mother's needlepoint
pillows. The floorboard's afternoon shine. You're
bored? So were they, so their boredom goes here
in the shellac and the veneer. Clock-makers too many
for the head of a pin. The guy who's embedded in
the haircut on my head. The transparent ones in sheet
glass. The solid individuals in sheet metal. The horde with
us in our bed. Lampshades for god's sake. Toothbrush:
who imagined it? Who made it? Paper bags!
The conception of love. Hands, minds, feet. All these
efforts, way beyond naming, to show up, eat.
You who made it. I give you the hand on my pen.

SOMETHING — NOTHING

Finally, on a park bench — dappled sun
through summer leaves, little birds
darting through them as though
threading a fragile and complicated
weaving of thoughts my fingers
are not deft enough to handle, but
that I can reflect on in a complicated
process descending from the folds
of my brain — I am glad to be good for
something as evening approaches.
The light and the dark play on me. I am
pure instrument: all reed, strings,
winds, drum. Everything has its way
with me. Nothing has happened. I have
waited so long for nothing to happen.

Brian Henry

ORCHESTRATING FLIGHT

Whom are we discussing? Oh, or whom would we be cursing?
The man who falls asleep at the wheel when the car
Is no auto but your portfolio – in the red,
In the red – or the man scrubbing the shell of the hull
With the wrong kind of brush – on the mend, at the bend –
Or the boy who's almost a man and resists that fact
With all the with he can muster?
                                            Mister, you've missed
The point, which is this: the angle of the plane as it
Ascends, cutting through the birds cutting through the wind
To carry all these people and the belongings
They've carried on to where they feel they really must go,
Be going.
            The song the engines play scares the men,
Scares the birds, the boy too caught up in his *hows*, *wheres*,
And *when*s to care if the plane might grind itself back to ground.

So, now. So, here. We know whom we are discussing. Oh, or
Whom we should be cursing. It's the boy! All one hundred
And twenty pounds of him. His velcro'd leather uppers,
His poly-cotton blend. His Walkman, his visor.
He's the one we'll blame when the plane goes down. His lack
Of concern, his inward, unpatriotic frown.
The posture – so poor – that shows us where he truly stands –
In the red, at the bend.
                            Only one loves a narcissist.
That is what we want to say. Your carry-on must fit
Beneath the seat in front of you is what he hears.
But he has no briefcase, no laptop. His bag so small
It hardly counts. Anyone could lift it, none use it
To float in the unlikely event of a water landing.
We say unlikely because below us there is no water.

Below us is land, land, and more land – almost red,
Before the mend. We think about that and how it blends
With what we hear, we tell ourselves we will not survive
A fall if this boy, that boy right there, does not pull out
Of himself soon enough to keep the hull of the auto
Of this plane in the red on the mend as it does
Its very very best to ascend.
                                        Above the birds!
With the men! With this boy at the bend!
                                                    Above the land!
In the red! With the shell on the mend!
                                                Above and with,
With and above: empathy, sympathy, and self-love.
Only one likes a narcissist. No one loves a plane.
Keep this in mind, dear boy whom we have come to hate.
To be in pain, or on its cusp, will not deliver us.
You must pull out of, or, oh how you emperil us.

INTERIOR: AIRPORT BAR

Parsimonious gesture, you're a sorry pickle,
Sliced and speared, a dent in my Bloody Mary.
Dog-eared lime, wedge of lemon: you will never get
To heaven. Every head at the bar knows the fiction
Called Operation Iraqi Freedom is a fiction.
Hemorrhoidal, blistered, the call to drink
Brings them – and me – to drink as fast as the mouths
Allow. The horror of pepper, of melting ice
That wrecks my alcoholic concoction. The horror
Of the horror, of the news we do not print
Or read. Add some sugar, some Sweet N Low
And see if the cocktail picks up, falls back,
Jumps forward, is bolted. It does not because it cannot.
I fall out of my chair. Or maybe I do not.

No one sitting at the bar lends a hand, each hand
Being preempted by a drink / by a cigarette.
All but one has a tropical complexion –
Leather soaked in a cocktailed concoction.
Add some salt, some Equal and the skin is a pickle,
Penurious gesture. But now it's time to return
To me, whose view from the floor affords a view
Of the ceiling – the tiles, the globes that pretend
To conceal cameras, the track lights and ducts that shine
And blow on the TV news we do not – no, we do.
We care, we care, we care. See, they squint to see
The person who is not a person but a fiction that falls back,
Bolts forward, is picked up, jumped. Each cell phone's ring
A prelude to Operation Desert Lynching.

But there there are no trees; it's all a fiction.
A fraction of the present view – bird's eye view –
The pilots of this establishment have procured.
It's a danger, the floor when wet, the bar at the bar
They breathe against, drain the sand from their drinks against.
They wring their spears from their concoctions, flustered
From the horror of the one who is not them floored –
Blistered gesture, gravid tincture. Not fit to print.
But fit to congeal, this sodden cocktail of a human.
Fit to peel – nothing like a lemon – and wrap
What has fallen back to be picked up, put forward – a dent –
Bolted upright and in an occupied position.
Quite a pickle, Operation Slice of Heaven. Quite a fiction.

97% OF THE POPULATION LIVE WITHIN FIVE MILES OF THE COAST

Was it there I saw the sea-like sea,
its recycling bin sneezed up
by every other swell?
Ragweed reaches this far – the wind –
my eyes so red,
           so red. They raw; close.

I've been told pink tissue is stuck,
                     in clumps,
to the stubble beneath my nose.
The wind leaves that part alone.
I've been told everyone loves a beach scene,
especially when the beach's name's not known.

I keep that in mind, will not reveal.
But might not be able to resist a hint
or two: there is no boardwalk, no pier;
my goddamn face is leaking, my sleeve
is streaked with snot.
               (I do not belong here.)

Keston Sutherland

LIVERY

That there is the humidity, that dumb licking
bacterium forked up is blood, is your own.
It cinches into that outline, is federal and day after
one day in a puce towel rots go blowfish crimper
crazy mated interred up and devastated by a
passion in its stages for that lip there is
                    this for you off-white
                    hot perfume bolted on
that calx gone soft, be famished for a touch that
perfect that analysed spite go snaps into
and act the descent of flesh livid uninterested
light scraped out from the puddle of darkness
to the shore where the shore massaged is about
that close to this lip outline. Throw in
                    your head to chew
                    it look xanthomonas be
it upset in the back garden make a way to
be that live with it, hot decay as the noise of losing
softens under this skin it infundibulum cap burnt
eyes in a crisp bag, in this fountain. Do you want
take this back, reel in an outline of what that is
that is left to die for next which trait which it is this
                    colour of yellow
                    them scraped out
picket in easy money burnt off, pick burning
now with a desire. At the right decency of flesh, cut
and repaired such a risible phoenix also then going
along with love, in one part chlorox nine
parts water running too late to wait thickened in
better again to catch it out the fire puts itself last
                    you know this
                    is the drill, drink up.

The highs don't last but neither does the withdrawal
race into their place, your life does this. Shit does
this abstract sift love into its acne scars you roll down
a window that there is your body take a reason
to live as it as this for granted, to stand as its blood in a grid
and shake your ass. But what is creosote
                            not for if you
                            that rocky descent to
bright tryptophan in piss, that fluctuations in the rate of
profit stimulate a crisis observable forever through
the pink glass of its display closet you lick you
stick it's that freezing but this ice now adequates to
the transmitter in correct mind damage. Blow this
torch out this hoover. In its outline, scrambling
                            begging away
                            its whole pivot to slap
bang in the relocated edge clutching to resort
that way to me, this sensation of an unintelligible
halt cannot getting your call in from a base
of a cone cannot wait on you the brushes in a tree
that that humidity screens out, waking
and taking turns its solitary gang-bang
                            repositioned across it that
                            car slide
slide it on dead, rip a line out.   The highs do
last the noise of losing dies away, this is your
own new blood take it. Ritornello yellow
and scraped, a shoplight withers over the syringe
and the air is anaclitic and the stars seen through
it dab it against this sciatica, and finally against
                            the wrong eye burning
                            like a ring of benzene.

So what do you drink yourself to death
just tired working hard appreciated however as
a runnel can death really be said to get any nearer
spits you in the vocoder, on the granulated march
fistule KBR extinction contract panicking to
too many clouds, too much queasy marine life
                              check this faucet rpm
                              nail the plastic bowls down
later to fold them up. You are a good helping and
you are told that in outline. Nearly enough
love today but the resentment of passion wasn't there
then was passion there is this it can you fold me
that up melatonin syringed into a more risible eel at
is scattering my flame fatuously, its dots on
                              top its leaves scar
                              take shit out for a meal
Parsons Corp. A deeper cracking and scraping noise
it is raining prawns are here now the right seat is up
take me to a night in the world, to get that lately free
of need look. It is indubitable that the Arabs want
gameshows just as in the foyer you said to me
that you wanted sexual happiness for the animals
                              stripped and lined up
                              in their diversity
constituting for us both a discouraging frieze of fur
but you did not say that they would get it
so will they get it. Forced conical stint palpation or
not you are what you are, try what you like
for nothing. In conclusion the pâté windowcleaner
door latch spring shit ice and water to be seen
                              with are these.
                              They'll get you in anywhere.

John Tranter

TRANSATLANTIC

Paris was not a place, it was the event,
and in that event the great writer
wrote about her grand obsession: herself.
Remember that the great writer liked
the evening telephone. The fade of age.

She said; snob strongly and snob often,
that was what she wanted.
If you go to the reading-rooms
as a result of smoking the herb of contempt
nothing you read will do you any good.
Why am I talking to you?

We received at least the evening sky
which was hers to inherit; that,
and a few thousand dollars.

My friendships after all, Helene said,
were based on direct emotion.
She did not stifle the great writer,
rather the work of the great writer
stifled others, a known council of vulgarisers.
You are journalists, Helene said,
you are all mechanical men.
Helene would be more inclined to violence, and
these *femmes de menage* stumbled into
a life filled with permanent anger.
Naturally it is a big explosion,
she yelled. You remember emotions.

The great writer had a mystic in to teach us
mysticism. He was attracted by Janet;
drop dead, Janet said. So he taught
moral tales, how ambition clogs the career.
Discretion is a kid of dilution, courtesy a limp.

O far shore, wrote the voice.

They met in the Luxembourg Gardens and
paperback in hand, turned to rend
what was left of my love story.
Oh those dark intellectual comments,
later printed in those Moral Tales.

There were traces in the enormous room
of what had made them.
Just stay here. We spent hours there.
To have lain with a little book.

Oh, drink, bring peace to the flesh.

Claire Crowther

NUDISTS

In the home of the naked, glass is queen.
A rule of sunlight on his left shoulder.
Her forearms hide a Caesarean scar

and a tied net curtain tries
to billow towards thighs that stray apart.
It serves a surprise to passers-by.

Nakedness is not the revelation
of glass. No less opaque than neighbours,
even after dark when she loosens

the long hair of voiles. He stops talking,
notices that the window is hung with one
slant reflection of them both, framed.

THE CITY OF TURNS

The sea rolled itself into a sweat
down our faces as if the tide
had suddenly thought of us as inlets

while radiant-crested, gorgeously-winged
dark-red and orange container crates
trembled from cranes on the dock

and a dead foal's eyes stared toward them
along a horizon striped with steel.
Ripples of sand spread to her mane,

relaxed as if from running. The dunes
hid other burials. I covered
the head with my shirt. My breasts,

salt quartz. Seagulls curfewed an eagle.
A shovel of wings packed him off
across this city of turns, the sea.

Julian Stannard

RINA'S FUNERAL

I stepped out of the Economics Faculty
only to be drenched by a summer storm.
No way I could catch a train like that.
So I took St. Anna's red-box funicular
and slipped my key into the apartment door:

rugs, table, our Malthusian fridge,
the umbrella I should have strapped to my leg.

I dried every part of myself as slowly as I could
and then lay down on the bed.

THE FUTURE

They gave me a pair of shoes
and told me to make them last.
They weren't the right size
and the colour, well the *colour* . . .
I reckoned with several tins
of brown polish I could give
them a brownish inflexion . . .
There was something about them
which made me think of
oil-tankers and corruption.
All the while *Leonard Cohen* was
singing from his latest album.
So I bet you can imagine
what a great time we were having.

Stuart Henson

VERLAINE IN CAMDEN

I

Dust, dust under the carriage-wheels
and in May the limes in the crescent
are shady and green with expectation.

In the heat of mid-day an old dog
lolls by the steps to a basement.
The children are indoors, the windows open.

The smells of these rooms will cling to their lives
like forgotten melodies, compelling and sweet:
a tincture of dry mould and camphor.

Tonight the moon will linger over the railway-arch,
languid as a woman in her bath. Someone will light
the first lamp in a window across the street.

Until then there is nothing to do but wait
for the water-cart as it passes, rattling like a hearse,
uttering its own impossible benediction.

II

Indolence is a disease. Whoever claimed
the dignity of labour was full of shit,
that I concede. Nevertheless, I am resolved
to quit the life of a cockroach and become –
useful? We must all pay the rent.

Leçons de Français, Latin, Littérature,
en français, par deux Gentlemen Parisiens . . .
No-one responds. The humiliation
of the personal advertisement.
In bed, I scan the *Echo* and the *Telegraph*.

THE SHAH OF PERSIA: STATE VISIT
We might dress up, provoke a policeman
into frisking us, thick-fingered,
and let him ignorantly touch
these cuts – stigmata – the flayed buttock.

Desire corrupts. (*Lust-object: anagram?*)
Rimbaud's a bastard got by Lucifer.
Face of an altar-boy, manners of a slut.
Ah, indolence! A slow rot, like gangrene.
The only cure is death – or God.

III

(French Lesson)

My name is Duval, Dufour . . . Armand, Maurice . . .
I am seeking comfortable and inexpensive accommodation.

There is weeping in my heart.
My companion is feeling a little unwell.

Your town is charming and full of amusements.
The sky is copper and void of all light.

I would like to know more of your customs and manners.
I am afraid of a kiss as of a bee.

Your soul is a chosen landscape.
I believe we may have met once – at the station.

The rain is gentle, on the earth and upon the roofs.
Do I understand myself? Do I understand nature?

I would like to purchase a fish and a bottle of oil.
To be worthy in action, upright in thought!

We were alone and walked dreaming.
How much is a one-way ticket to Brussels?

Your name is Armand, Maurice . . . Duval, Dufour . . .
I would like to purchase a pistol and fifty rounds
                                                    of ammunition.

Arthur Rimbaud

from ILLUMINATIONS

CHILDHOOD

I

That idol, black-eyed, yellow-maned, no kin, no court, nobler than fable, Mexican and Flemish: his domain – insolent green and azure – extends along beaches with fiercely Greek, or Slav, or Celtic names given them by unnavigable waves.

At the forest's edge – dream flowers jangle, split and flare – the girl with orange lips: her knees crossed in the clear spate pouring from the meadows, her nakedness shaded, traversed and clothed by rainbows, flora, sea.

Ladies circling on the terraces beside the sea; girls and giant-esses, superbly black against the grey-green moss, jewels set proud on the rich soil of the groves and little gardens after thaw – young mothers, older sisters, eyes brimming with pilgrimage, wives of Sultans, princesses of tyranny in their dress and their bearing, diminutive foreign women, people full of unpretentious sadness.

How trying when it comes, the moment for the routine kiss, the mechanical fondness.

II

That's her, the little dead girl behind the roses. – The youthful mamma, also dead, comes down the steps. – The cousin's carriage rasps on the sand. – There's the younger brother (away in the Indies!), with the sunset backdrop, on the field of pinks. – The old men buried upright in the rampart of wallflowers.

The swarm of golden leaves encircles the general's quarters. They're down in the South. – You take the red road till you come to the disused inn. The grand house is for sale; its shutters are falling off. – The priest must have removed the key to the church. – The keepers' lodges on the estate are empty. The rustling treetops are all you glimpse over the tall fences. Nothing to be seen in there anyhow.

The fields slope up to villages without cockerels or anvils. The sluice gates are shut. Oh the Calvaries, the mills turning in the wilderness, the islands and hayricks!

A droning of magical flowers. And *him* – rocked by the slopes. Beasts on the prowl, fabulously suave. Clouds massing above the high sea, an eternity of warm tears.

III

In the wood there is a bird; you stop and blush at its song.

There is a clock which doesn't strike.

There is a dip in the ground with a nest of white animals.

There is a descending cathedral and a rising lake.

There is a little car abandoned in the copse, or coming down the lane, covered in ribbons.

There is a troupe of little actors, in costume, spotted on the road through the edge of the wood.

There is someone, finally, to chase you away when you're tired and thirsty.

IV

I am the saint praying on the terrace – as the meek animals graze down to the Sea of Palestine.

I am the scholar in the dark armchair. Rain and foliage batter at the library window.

I am the traveller on the high road through the stunted trees; the sound of the lock-water drowns my footsteps. For a good while I watch the melancholy, golden wash of sunset.

I could well be the child abandoned on the jetty, torn away and heading out to sea, the little servant boy following the lane which crests in the sky

The paths are rough. Broom grows on the hillocks. The air is still. The birds seem so distant, and the springs! If you keep going, it can only be the end of the world.

V

They can rent me out this tomb, then, with cement lines picked out on whitewash – very deep in the ground.

I plant my elbows on the table, the lamplight glares on these newspapers which I'm an idiot to reread, and these mediocre books.

Way above my earth-walled sitting room, houses spread their roots, mists convene. The mud is red or black. Monstrous city, night without end!

Slightly nearer are the sewers. All around, only the thickness of the globe. Chasms of azure maybe, wells of fire. It's perhaps at these levels that moons clash with comets, or oceans with fables.

In more bitter moments, I imagine balls of sapphire, or metal. I'm master of the silence. What is that feeble gleam at the corner of the ceiling-vault, like light through a vent?

LIVES

I

Oh the vast avenues of the holy land, the terraces of the temple! What became of the Brahmin who explained the Proverbs to me? I can even see the old women, from that time, in that place! I remember hours of silver and sunlight, near the river, the landscape with its arm around my shoulder, our caresses, as we stood on the spiced plains. – A flock of scarlet pigeons thunders around my thoughts. – Exiled now, I once had a stage on which to perform the great dramatic works of all literatures. I could show you unbelievable riches. I duly acknowledge the history of the treasures you unearthed. I know what comes next! My wisdom is held in the same contempt as chaos. What is my nothingness, compared to the stupor that awaits you?

II

My merits as an inventor are quite different from those of my predecessors – a musician, you could venture, who has discovered something like the key of love. Presently a member of the landed gentry, in harsh countryside under sober skies, I should like to wax emotional about the memory of my pauper childhood, of an apprenticeship and turning up in clogs, of controversy, of five or six widowings and several wild sessions when a strong head kept me back from the fullness of pitch attained by my fellow drinkers. I don't regret my erstwhile share of divine high spirits: the sober air of this harsh landscape feeds my atrocious scepticism all too well. But since that scepticism no longer serves any purpose, and because I am now in the grip of a new uneasiness, I suspect my impending madness will be very ugly.

III

Shut up in an attic at the age of twelve, I came to know the world; I illustrated the human comedy. I learned my history in a store room. At some night-time festival in a Northern city, I met all the wives and women of the old painters. In a crumbling Paris backstreet, I was taught the classical sciences. In a magnificent dwelling surrounded by the entire Orient I completed my vast opus and sat out my illustrious retirement. I stirred my blood up. I have been relieved of my responsibilities. No point even thinking about them. I am really from beyond the grave; no debts outstanding.

Translated by Jeremy Harding

Anthony Barnett

The missing u in arab q

The missing u in arab q
Does not mean one would wait
Among the less than few in the early evening rain
Until you came along again, again, again too late

MESSAGE TO SEE ONE

And what is two thousand
And four for if not to write
If not to paint

And so to live and love

LETTER

To take heart
For this writing lark
The brain bereft
Of what is left

'sea discourages me, too big, too classic,
too much "best-seller"'

TEARFULLY, FEARFULLY

He lives timelessly
Although time must
Be passing because
He is tearfully fearfully aware
That it does

He feels he must be staying put

From midnight to daylight

Love lies lovelier
Than any rhyme

As good as his word

What have I done or not done

What have I done or not done
Willingly willfully
Setting down some circumlocution
Saying this is
What I want and do not want

Flashlight
Immersed in what I cannot see
Consciously afflicted
Light

On that day we travelled to a clearing beside a road and began to
walk along a narrow path that overlooked a clear swift flowing river

Unceremoniously centered

A LAST WORD IN YOUR EAR

As Allah decreed I dismounted
Clasped my arms around him and
Plunged a knife from my sleeve
Into his back as he also did to me

Aaggaa

Gill Gregory

THE RETURN OF THE HERD

(after Pieter Bruegel the Elder)

He understands their drift
implies a favour
filtered through –

a close-knit dream
or pattern of arrival:

the reddish lane,
warm hearts
in age approved.

His autumn frames my fear
(stoic in the trees) –

a rust-stained line
of living things

if I'm not deceived.

Caitriona O'Reilly

DUETS

Underneath, her voice is
a whalebone-and-cambric
arrangement, a set of stiff stays

or pegs, well-hammered-in.
She is a house with firm foundations.
Her fabric pulls apart

in the upper floors only,
where something can be heard
fluttering with calculated frailty,

a coquette's attenuated eyelash
or lace-fringed can-can dress,
a spinning coin dropped

on a polished table,
an ornamental dove trapped
in an attic, beating tired wings.

Her voice has entered every corner of itself.
The boy's voice is an arrow pointing upwards.
Its flute-notes issue from an instrument

still half a sapling, with green feet in the ground
and a flicker of leaves around its crown.
It has the gothic hollowness

of cathedral pipes, a cylindrical sound,
which is the shape a boy's voice makes
crossing its own vast space.

Stuart Calton

STANDARD LIFE

I

Look at this expert false
hope its intermittent
light rotates the coast, un-
            mistakable and
eating burdens nationally.
Skin nukes out like strangle
happy Nazi or have a
            proper natural
thought like neon
            gets hot and
bottoms out, whisks
            bricks or the
North had a stroke
            like we saw
pay-out throat knife
            scab open a
Co-op. A crushed bowler so
            smoulders breathe
fire, wisely, half-clad,
            satellite stench
enlightenment roars down screaming
            hunks of grey
slag, caps your New Harmony credit
            round-a-bout put
bubble-wrap or in Blackburn.
            I don't know,
            Skelmersdale.

            Guess or come
            off it now can
chunk through the brûlée the
exploding web of piled sand
put pipes up or go
            bust or
suffer the full collapse at
least robust and less and
glare at your left arm believed
            red can
not allow ongoing risk-shoots
and pushing a fall opposition
surge, it's won.

II

Tell me of your
            satellite broach
whip caught on
            mill-pond revenue
branches, flay the
            ground salted
fields splashing and buy
            a couple then, utterly
foxed. The war-paint of the
Venezuelan middle-class is
toothpaste supposed to dim or
            spend effect tear-gas
ground-weed rubbed on the blade tell
me of your Robert Owen prop up
Visa product. Light industrial ribbons colour-
            fast non-provision of
trisected unitary river-mass vital needs
spit it off. Quicklime. Yeah, and lay it on
like soda, lust-effect ashen.

The eight-hour hen look
sharp and they cap down a
market poker in this case too
            non-contributory, expect this
increase, filter what's competitive up with
your gullet, locked to a cut
rate trunk gets really distinctive.
            So against him should be
dropped, present and now we
triumph, soapy knots lash
            out on breaded meat.

Pick up a mouse,
            locked out
of which smash
            open this polish wide
buck we fought
            and won.

Jane Routh

ELEVENTH HOUR

There are leaves still on the trees
near the mountain hut, Mont Blanc framed
perfect against blue sky. In Yellowstone
you can see only stars. It's night
in Auckland too: those are its lights
glittering across the bay from Devonport.

The South Pole's out of action, all turbulence
and wind. Mawson Station's on:
portacabins in primaries, rock, snowdrifts.
No one outside. Pale sky almost green.
Ascencion looks abandoned: 27° – dawn I think –
a white dory pulled up the hard, a wave.

Macquarie's frozen, a Sisley of lilac
greys and green, but Antarctica's left behind
its sound effects: sea ice breaks and cracks
unstoppably, a Weddell seal yawns.
Nothing from Nuuk; and in the dark, Denali's
lost to Anchorage's light pollution.

Ah yes. Bagdhad. Out-of-date
as you'd expect. A green shop sign,
an ordinary side-street. No one's about.
The text is Spanish – if I have it right, it says
all people are collaterals.
Everyone. Everywhere.

Armistice Day 2003

ALL MY DEAD

The lately-dead return in the night, balance
their over-large heads on thin bones and ask
Do you think I am going to die? Yes, I say, Yes.
Their faces are crumpled like a newborn's.
I hear them screaming under the bed.
It is not easy to imagine what it is like
to exist only in someone else's memory.

The long-dead are quieter. They leave their toils
in ones and twos, step up to say their names.
Sometimes they bring a landscape with them.
Souls of their dead infants cling to the women's skirts
like patchy fog; even they do not remember
their faces. Subsistence is what they care about:
they do not mind what you invent.

And those not-yet-dead who know they
are next in line, the ones with grandchildren,
make ready, and talk among themselves about
how someone should have photographed
the moor before it was fenced, or haytime even:
this is the closest they come to saying
what they mean. Then they start to repeat themselves.

Philip Rush

WABI SABI

The windfalls are rotting
on the burnt grass.
He cannot decide whether he should

photograph them or not.

Sam Gardiner

THE BEST

The best are snowmen crying in the rain
in tiny gardens, where cars stand nose to nose,
bonnets raised for the kiss of life, ready
to show a clean pair of wheels before running
out of road, or years, and ordering bored
kids in the back to count the little corpses:
two hedgehogs, three pheasants, one badger.
The best are the lost, binned by ditched lovers,
or bounced off lorries rounding Devils' Elbows
where hills rub shoulders and phoneboxes are roofed
with solar panels. 'Best' is greatest, fastest,
most, and never enough, but better is gentler,
quieter, less athletic, and plainly better.
The best make no sport of competition,
are best at losing games of let's pretend,
score no goals, breast no tapes, trample hurdles,
drop the egg, and probably the spoon as well,
and do not bother commentators or measurers
or rulebooks agreed for the sake of argument.
They detox history by letting it pass without
a *Take that!*: third degree caustication for lack
of precedence (those past years of Dinky Toys
if saved would now be worth a fortune), a stone
at the window, an injection of bullets for 1690.
Of each it can be said that he or she
is one of the best of watchers and listeners
(dear God, please send us a new television).
They need boast no roots (weeds have roots) and when
the naked field maple, trunk as tight as
a shut book, slowly bursts into sticky buds,
crooks its knuckles against the glass and asks for
a field to throw wide its arms in, even they
once came next door to borrow long armed loppers,

and by dusk their garden was full of limbs.
Equal among the best is one (A) who rushes
across a trembling footbridge across a tributary
that rushes to join a river, the banks of which
are lined with poets skipping stones on the water,
and taking notes, one (B) who is averse
to taking sides by drawing in two dimensions
a contentious pippin with one or two sides
short of infinity, and one (C) trapped by a desk,
addressing different words, that make no difference,
to an empty room and to the emptiness
beyond, the laptop blinking back a tear
and the printer being sick in the corner.

N. S. Thompson

IN A NORTHERN TOWN

I

How could you put it in perspective? In the long perspective of a Northern town? Hard cantons of sloping rooftops, backyards, washhouses whitewashed by a line of washing. What could you say? What could you see beyond the slope of moorland rising to a monumental folly? Feel moving in a line of traffic by the soot-black century of a parish church? On the corner by the cemetery?

Warm contours of the South. Brake of poplars in the still blue air leading over cobblestones to a line of graves.

Terra cotta pantiles. Bodies ripe and biscuit brown. Vines along a terrace, tumbling over washing lines and a rusting mangle on a washhouse floor. How could you put them in perspective?

II

Eyes waking in a whitewashed room,
mind washed by tides of wine, beside
the shoreline of a body, you
gazed on a populated world:

an arctic place where peaks of slate
shone abstract from a wall of ice
and capped the frozen crags of shops
with flats in antique stone and grit.

Love trickled in your mind. Canals
dreamed by a flow of industry
and disappeared round a curve
where steep mills like a mirror gleamed.

Much later, sitting in the park,
you saw the mystery below
stone walls, where blades of grass in shells
of ice preserved your still green world.

III

A land obedient, not kind; the people not obedient, but kind, performing everything expected of them: dutiful in mill and office block, minds elsewhere. A radio, perhaps a song, along its mercantile streets, where columns of municipal lighting went, fine fluting supporting the appeal to industry, proclaimed along the peristyles of bank and public building, *rococo* cupola of an indoor market hall, the decorated style of a department store.

And as you pulled out of ornamental streets, a flower bed revealed as coat of arms arose emblazoned from the diamond chains ringing the statues of monarch, statesman and manufacturing millionaire.

The ornamental world. Monumental in its folly.

How could you put it in perspective?

IV

The low brow of a distant hill seen from
The window said it all, a winding road
Out to the far horizon, where the sky's
Visceral tissue gleamed transparently,
Arching a rainbow blue in light: you felt
Earth curve beneath you, saw slow bends in time.

V

But time seemed dead.
Turmoil of weeds among unending brick.

The cargo of antique world. Its shells of factories, strings of mills,
tiled *art deco* buildings boarded up down cobbled streets, invaded by
weather, survived against the weather. A world devoid of ideas. Ideas
devoid of a world.
The space and waste of industrial zones.
Clouds that disappeared in the upper atmosphere.

Where would you find the gods and goddesses
Or row of vines along a terraced street?

VI

And in that world, a solitary hour
Behind the broken backs of houses, sheds
And chimney pots that grow a single flower,
You wondered what went on inside the heads
There: rows of houses looking singular
With statues, bird baths, nymphs and rotting car.

VII

She suffered all the passion afternoons
Could summon up and down excited nerves,
But laughed once you had dared to take a peep:
The sheet found stamped with smiles of crescent moons
Drily describing in the shape of curves
Two eyes drawn in the comic act of sleep.

*

Among the curricula of the city and its sophisticated outposts, time accelerated to become rooms filled with smoke and people, who dreamed in fashions of the minute as conversations seeped and drained, words sinking into porous time, individuals testing their fabric against time woven by men and women.

The rooms soon cracked. The carpets threadbare.

Why the pretence at permanence?

*

VIII

Triumphant in each other's arms, you lay
Protracted while the lambent moon
Increased its angle on you in the sky

Peering through what had been a normal day
To furrowed sheets, late afternoon,
And caught you in the cold light wondering why.

*

Cinder tracks led by the school, by railings of a railway line and tracks along the memory. Immensities of blue swam round the pallor of an ashen daytime moon.

A playground stark against stone mills. Cast cinders by cast iron.

Ancient factories spun lines of mirrors, ascending to a sky refracted as an endless skein of light, and windows gleaming like a line of ancient poetry. Spondee and dactyl. Or a catalectic. Cataleptic.

You paused for interlude.

IX

Leaf-veined, the moon does not requite
When scenic nymphs go underground:
Diana hunts alone, love slips from sight.

*

Curved white moons bathing in blue day
Provoke spring blossom, nascent greens,
Snare mating beast and man to hunt: feet splay.

*

A pearl moon set in summer sky
And rich gold fields now drunk with wine-dark blood
Protests its innocence. The firm young wheat waves dry.

*

Moon gaping, ruddy like a toping mouth,
Sits on a vintage newly pressed in bloated vat.
A ploughman tills dark fields. The homeward crane winds south.

X

And in that moment, life lifts its skirts to you: rising over rooftops, in a stolen hour, flashing as cold light in columns of air, sun's highlighting on streets of damp pavements, railings; telephone wires and a distant railway line wet-gleaming beyond fields, patterns emerge along the slow trail of a star, the plant and its parts.

*

Walking the winter white streets, you whistle. Voices call out on the frosted air, across fields, over pavements on housing estates. A world unfolds, then folds you in its arms.

A terrace. Moorland. An empty space in worlds orbiting around stone. Secrets of birth, perception. First love, first words, first world.

Hills of heather. Blackberries.

A low intensity. A calmness.

An earthly propensity.

*

All causation runs along the kaleidoscope of time, turns to a handful of clockwork hours. The only definition lies in those points of time in the sleeping buds called memories.

Howard Wright

SOMERVILLE

The air is still. Chlorophyll stifles goosegrass and nettles,
the great trees glowing above the low-water glitter . . .
Suddenly a hawk is pinned and wriggling to the sky's blue breast,
and you can keep it in sight from the deranged bike
as you overtake the bra-less woman pushing a tireless baby
and bags of goods in a shopping trolley along the cycle path.
Nobody, least of all you, wants to be a freewheeler all their life.
The hawk drops as if winged, and a search party of cattle
fans out, intent on blood and feathers, so missing
the jet-glint break its connections to the infinite and plummet
to the fine line between heaven and hell . . . You are heading
that way, easily by the shortest route, measuring time
by the beat of the pedals and space by the mangled butterflies,
leaving the consumerist pieta of mother and child
to the mercies of underpasses, defenceless playgrounds,
and the *Lili Marlene* and *Greensleeves* of the ice-cream van
when it goes visiting the cardboard houses in silent estates.

Essays

The *Poetry Review* Essay

JAN MONTEFIORE

Women and Tradition

We are, I am, you are
by cowardice or courage
the one who find our way
back to this scene
carrying a knife, a camera
a book of myths
in which
our names do not appear.

The resonant ending of Adrienne Rich's "Diving into the Wreck" (1975), about her quest into oceanic depths in search of something lost (her unconscious self? a vanished collective history?), intimates that the woman poet was doing something lonely, difficult and dangerous. In the earlier "Snapshots of a Daughter-in-Law" Rich had raged at the way women's poetry was flawed by being marginalized, so that potential geniuses like Emily Dickinson allowed themselves to be brilliant amateurs – "mere talent was enough for us / glitter in fragments and rough drafts" – or let their work be seared by their own frustration and fury, "reading while waiting for the iron to heat / Writing *My Life had stood – a loaded Gun* / In that Amherst pantry, while the jellies boil and scum". Those seething preserves clearly represent a domestic hunger, rebellion, and rage which, as in Virginia Woolf's *A Room Of One's Own*, are seen as damaging flaws. And the woman poet was not just lonely and frustrated; as Rich argued in the influential essay "When We Dead Awaken" (1971), she would find that tradition, that "book in which our names do not appear", would be no help but rather an obstacle to the girl or woman who tried to write:

> She goes to poetry or fiction looking for her way of being in the world, since she too has been putting words and images together; she is look-ing eagerly for guides, maps, possibilities; and over and over in the

"masculine persuasive force" of literature she comes up against something that negates everything she is about: she meets the image of Woman in books written by men. She finds a terror and a dream, she finds "La Belle Dame Sans Merci", she finds a beautiful pale face, she finds Juliet or Tess or Salomé, but precisely what she does not find is that absorbed, drudging, puzzled, sometimes inspired creature, herself, who sits at a desk trying to put words together.

John Donne's "masculine persuasive force" (the quote is from "To His Mistris" – "By our first strange and fatal interview...") epitomises the damaging presumption of the great tradition of English poetry, "that men wrote poems and women appeared in them". Or as I put it in *Feminism and Poetry* (1987), "Women have a paradoxical relationship to tradition. As readers and writers we belong to it, but as women we are excluded.... Our exclusion takes the forms of misinterpretation and of simple omission". I was thinking when I wrote the latter of my own experience of education in English Literature, at school where we studied no women writers except Jane Austen (I learned of Christina Rossetti and Mary Sidney by poring over my hymnbook during the *longueurs* of school prayers), at Oxford where I studied no woman writer for my finals at all, and as a university teacher of canonical English Literature which included women novelists but no poets except for Emily Dickinson. (Though I was and remain sceptical that the poets' representations of women are as major a problem as all that to the would-be woman poet; to me now, as when I wrote *Feminism and Poetry*, "the common-sense objection that having the time and space to write in, being able to talk to or at least correspond with fellow-writers, and having access to the means of publication, are more influential than the deterrent effects of Milton, Wordsworth & Co., carry a lot of weight." There are many worse ways of oppressing people than teaching them *Paradise Lost*.)

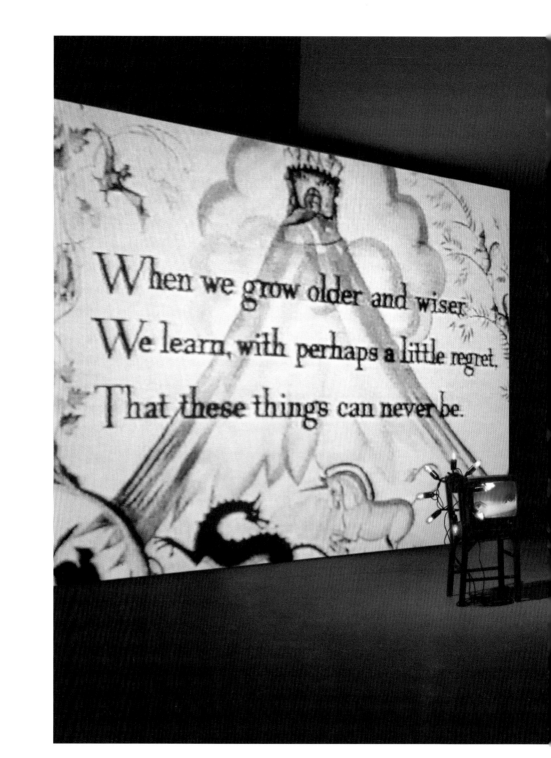

In any case that was then in the 1970s, a generation ago, and this is now: *nous avons changé tout cela.* It seems improbable that potential women writers are still frightened off their vocations by the apparition of "La Belle Dame Sans Merci" when they are as likely to be studying Carol Ann Duffy as Keats for A-level, and when any university course they take in Romanticism is certain to feature Mary Shelley's *Frankenstein*. English poetry is not today taught or understood as a single "Great Tradition" of mastery and magnificence, but as several intertwined traditions, in which women's poetry often features. Thus accounts of and courses in English Renaissance poetry will now include Aemilia Lanier's *Salve Rex deus Judaeorum* (1611) with its defences of Pilate's wife, Daughters of Jerusalem, Eve and Mary Magdalen, and Mary Sidney's transformations of the Psalms into lyric meditations. Religious poetry seems to have attracted women because although there certainly are traditions of Judaeo-Christian antifeminism, the soul's relation to God is not determined by gender – as is unobtrusively emphasised in Mary Sidney's version of Psalm 139: "My bones are not hid from thee. …Thine eyes did see my substance, yet being imperfect":

> Thou, how my back was beam-wise laid,
>   And raft'ring of my ribs dost know:
>   Know'st ev'ry point
>   And ev'ry joint,
>   How to this whole the parts did grow
> In brave embroid'ry fair arrayed
>   Though wrought in shop both dark and low.
>
> Nay, fashionless, ere form I took,
>   Thy all and more beholding eye
>   My shapeless shape
>   Could not escape
>   All these time framed successively,
> Ere one had being, in the book
>   Of thy foresight enrolled did lie.

But the changes made in the canon of poetry as taught in schools and universities as a result of pressure by feminist-influenced scholarship and criticism are only indirectly important for contemporary poets. The question remains: how have women poets situated themselves in relation to their available tradition(s)?

One answer is that that women poets (re)invent the past, as in Elizabeth Bishop's early comi-tragic lyric "Casabianca":

Love's the boy stood on the burning deck
trying to recite 'The boy stood on
the burning deck.' Love's the son
    stood stammering elocution
     while the poor ship in flames went down.

Love's the obstinate boy, the ship,
even the swimming sailors, who
would like a schoolroom platform, too
    or an excuse to stay
    on deck. And love's the burning boy.

This apparently light, baffling poem half-parodies, half-repeats a once-famous recitation piece about a "beautiful and bright" youth who stubbornly obeyed the orders of his father, who unknown to him had already been killed. The heroic boy's obstinacy and the obedient pupil's repetitive stammering seem to epitomise fixed and damaging patterns of inhibition, yet the final phrase powerfully suggests a fiery eroticism: Ovid and Anacreon are invoked here quite as much as Felicia Hemans, author of the original "Casabianca".

But more frequent than lyricism is storytelling. In *Feminism and Poetry* I looked at the way some women poets, notably Stevie Smith, Liz Lochhead in *The Grimm Sisters*, and Anne Sexton in *Transformations*, chose to situate themselves at an angle to tradition by writing poems which are based on but critical of traditional stories. This strategy I found attractive if finally limited because "political reinterpretations can deflect but not alter [traditional] meanings, which either return to haunt the poem that discards them or vanish into witty analysis". The reinterpreted folk-tale or myth has famously become a feature of feminist poetry. It is handled with skill by Liz Lochhead in "Dreaming Frankenstein", a tripartite poem which starts with Mary Shelley's story of possession by nightmare:

This was the penetration
Of the seven swallowed apple pips.
Or else he'd slipped like a silver dagger
between her ribs and healed her up secretly
again. Anyway
he was inside her
and getting him out again
would be agony fit to quarter her
unstitching everything

In parts 2 and 3, this sympathetic third-person omniscience turns into ventriloquy: the monster speaking his sad exile ("The blind man did not hate me") and his viciously homoerotic creator/lover/persecutor ("What wouldn't you / give to love me. An arm, and a leg? / Going to make you. / Make you sit up and / beg"). The effect is similar to U. A. Fanthorpe's well-known "Not My Best Side", which re-tells the tale of St George and the Dragon in the voices of the dragon, the maiden and the knight as portrayed by the painter Uccello. The most interesting of these re-tellings do not change the morals of well-known tales so much as open up different spaces in them, like Fanthorpe's quirky monologues of minor Shakespearian female characters about to come to sticky ends: for instance the "Waiting Gentlewoman" in *Macbeth*:

> HM's a super person, of course,
> But she's a bit seedy just now,
> Quite different from how marvellous she was
> At the Coronation. And this doctor they've got in –
> Well, he's only an ordinary little G.P.,
> With a very odd accent, and even I
> Can see that what HM needs is
> A real psychiatrist. I mean, all this
> About *blood*, and *washing*. Definitely Freudian.

But Fanthorpe's "take" on tradition and myth is many-sided, and not only preoccupied with gender issues. Thus her sequence about death, "Stations Underground", moves lightly between contemporary England and classical mythology, as in the numinous "Rising Damp", with its italicized four-beat, falling interjections about the forgotten rivers of London – and elsewhere:

> Being of our world, they will return
> (Westbourne, caged at Sloane Square
> Will jack from his box),
> Will deluge cellars, detonate manholes,
> Plant effluent in our faces,
> Sink the city.
>
> *Effra, Graveney, Falcon, Quaggy,*
> *Wandle, Walbrook, Tyburn, Fleet*
>
> It is the other rivers that lie
> Lower, that touch us only in dreams

That never surface. We feel their tug
As a dowser's rod bends to the source below

Phlegethon, Acheron, Lethe, Styx.

Less impressive is Carol Ann Duffy's satirical collection *The World's Wife*, which for all the rave reviews seems to me to suffer from a jokiness that palls, much like Terry Deary's *Horrible Histories* in verse. Duffy's technique of mediating an archaic situation through a modern woman's mind and idiom, which worked so well in her monologue "Standing Female Nude", becomes monotonous in the griping of Mrs Midas ("What gets me now is not the idiocy or greed / but lack of thought for me"), Mrs Aesop ("By Christ, he could bore for Purgatory"), Mrs Zeus, Mrs Faust, & Co., while the inverted stereotypes – "Queen Herod" having the potential rivals to her darling daughter killed off, or Queen Kong "peeping in at his skyscraper room / and seeing him fast asleep" – are a bit, well, obvious.

If it is true that the woman poet finds herself unable to use traditional forms of poetic rhetoric straightforwardly, like Virginia Woolf walking down Whitehall and finding herself "an outsider, alien and critical", then this is surely more of an asset than a limitation. Such critical sharpness certainly seems to inflect and strengthen the language of Jo Shapcott's lovely sequence of poems *The Roses (after Rilke)*, where the contemplated feminine rose answers the poet back:

I'm an imperfect thing,
neat, layered
but spilling petals and pollen,
dropping bruised scent

on to the ground.
Essence of roses is not sweet,
but brown at the edges
like the air you breathe.

**

Space folds against space,
petal touches petal;
you look at me
as though you want to fall in,

make the flower
glow with your own image,
change my meaning
from rose to Narcissus.

Another aspect of the woman poet's relation to tradition is the increasing invocation of the rhetoric of domesticity. This is not an invention of contemporary poets; Emily Dickinson could use cups kept safe on shelves to represent frustration, and Elizabeth Barrett Browning famously called on the "woman's figure" of needlework: "When / I speak, you'll take the meaning as it is, / And not allow for puckerings in the silks, / By clever stitches. I'm a woman, sir / I use the woman's figures, naturally". Nevertheless, since Sylvia Plath published "Mary's Song" which makes Holocaust poetry out of a roasting joint – "The Sunday lamb cracks in its fat" – women poets have deployed the imagery of domestic skills and crafts with increasing assurance and power, most often as an ambiguous image of the poet's desire to transcend time. In "Letter from a Far Country", by Gillian Clarke, for instance, the poet lovingly and ironically names her preserves, aware of the limitations of the kitchen:

Seville orange marmalade
anually staining gold
the snows of January

(The saucers of marmalade
are set when the amber wrinkles
like the sea when you blow on it)

...You can see the fruit pressing
their little faces against the glass;
tiny onions imprisoned
in their preservative juices

This celebration of skills already archaic in a world of supermarkets and deep freezers is also an elegy for their disappearance, now that the women are leaving:

They are paying their taxes
and dues. Filling in their passports.
They are paying to Caesar
what is Caesar's, to God what is God's.
To Woman what is Man's.

The "far country" is then both the old realm of domestic certainties in which the poet once lived and the new world of space and freedom which is open to her – at a price. There is a similar evocation of an era of domestic pastoral, which the poet at once yearns for and is relieved not to have to belong to, in Eavan Boland's sequence "Outside History", especially in the elegiac poem "What We Lost". Here a woman sewing in her kitchen by candlelight tells stories to "a child, who is my mother" who listens entranced but then gets up, moves away and forgets:

> The dumb-show of legend has become language,
> is becoming silence and who will know that once
>
> words were possibilities and disappointments,
> were scented closets filled with love-letters
> and memories and lavender hemmed into muslin,
> stored in sachets, aired in bed-linen
>
> and travelled silks and the tones of cotton
> tautened into bodices, subtly shaped by breathing?

Yet the complementary converse of such celebrations of domestic pastoral is the knowledge of mortality, the lavender bags scattered and the breathing stopped. So for the Jewish poet Lotte Kramer domestic imagery represents not continuity but loss, as in "Tablecloth" which sees this treasured family relic as the perishing token of a vanished world, its threads fraying

> In places, as in dreams
> When falling into pits
> We wake in unbelief.

Kramer's elegy for a fraying fabric does not only mourn the imminent passing of her own "disappeared" Jewish family from living memory; it also intimates that the domestic traditions represented by such treasured possessions have become threadbare fictions, which we yet need in order to go on living. It is increasingly plain that literary traditions whether domestic, religious or classical, are not so much obstacles to women poets as sources which enable them both to invoke numinous intertextual riches and to signal ironic dissent.

✍

A changed other person

PETER ROBINSON

W. S. Graham, *New Collected Poems*, edited by Matthew Francis
with a foreword by Douglas Dunn, Faber, £25, ISBN 0571210155

Clive Wilmer's poem "W. S. Graham Reading" describes the poet in old
age at Heffers bookshop, Cambridge, unable to fix on a single work
from his *Collected Poems* 1942–1977 (1979) which he wanted to read:
"as if to surrender to a single instance / of language / was to surrender". It was
an embarrassing moment for the event's organizers. The poet either drunk or
badly hung-over, the reading stalled, the small crowd's patience no more than
could be expected:

> Then: "Read any one of them," somebody cried:
> "they're all marvellous!"
> > And we beheld a marvel:
> an Archangel
> > a little damaged
> igniting the dark firmament with speech.

I can vouch for the documentary accuracy of Wilmer's poem. I was there.
But I confess it wasn't me who called out that unsolicited testimonial, and
confess too that I neither think Graham and his work quite deserving of
Coleridge's "damaged archangel" epithet, nor that "they're all marvellous" is
the true story of his poetry. Matthew Francis begins his editor's Introduction
to the recently published *New Collected Poems*: "Admirers of W. S. Graham
have long felt that his *Collected Poems* is due for revision." He is certainly a
poet whose work deserves to be available in full, or at least in a more
substantial volume than the 250-page selection that he assembled himself.
There's always a question, though, about what "in full" might entail. Francis
notes that "the present collection makes no claim to be a *Complete Poems*, but
I believe it does contain his best and most representative work".

A loaded contrast with Philip Larkin, whose *The Less Deceived* (1955)
was published in the same year as Graham's *The Nightfishing*, has dogged
criticism over the last twenty years or so. Douglas Dunn rightly insists on the
petty irrelevance of any such needing to choose between them in his foreword
to the volume: "There are different kinds of poetry and they are all indispen-
sable." The organization of Francis's *New Collected Poems* is, though, unlikely

to cause the controversy that Anthony Thwaite's Larkin *Collected Poems* (1988) did. Francis restores the integrity of Graham's individual collections. The poet failed to collect his first composed – though second published – book, *The Seven Journeys* (1944), and he cut poems from his first three acknowledged collections. His editor brings these back into print. He also dispenses with Graham's eccentric method of producing a contents list by numbering the poems collected and merely noting the names of the individual books from which they are taken as an afterthought. Nevertheless, the qualm remains. Graham, for whatever reason, thought the ones he excluded weren't as "marvellous" as those he put back into print.

At the other end of his *oeuvre* there are three broad categories of out-take. First, there are poems that Graham published but didn't collect, and which were released in a small press *Uncollected Poems* (1991), plus one from a back issue of *Stand* included in *Selected Poems* (1996). Secondly, we find unpublished poems that were rescued from notebooks sold for a monthly maintenance cheque to Robin Skelton in Canada and which appeared in *Aimed at Nobody* (1993). Then, thirdly, there are various others gathered from letters and manuscripts by Francis, including "*from* With the Dulle Griet in Canada" – an ambitious, but troubled, late attempt at a long poem connected with his 1973 reading tour. Dunn notes that the "repetition of 'language' and communication as obsessive, unfinished subjects can at times feel overdone". Graham being a poet with a handful of obsessive themes, the later poems he didn't collect do tend to be variations on matters handled in pieces that he did.

Take, for example, "Falling into the Sea" (first published 1977) and drawn from *Uncollected Poems*. It's an advice poem about how to enjoy drowning ("Breathing water is easy / If you put your mind to it") and ends:

> What has happened to you?
>
> You have arrived on the sea
> Floor and a lady comes out
> From the Great Kelp Wood
> And gives you some scones and a cup
> Of tea and asks you
> If you come here often.

I'm not sure what's happened to "you", but what's happened to the poem is that it's descended from the disturbingly unreal to the merely whimsical. In the official canon of 103 poems that Graham collected, this drowning obsession is well represented, in "Three Poems of Drowning", for instance, from *The White Threshold* (1949), a collection whose title announces the centrality of the topic. In "The Nightfishing", it is crossed with the language theme. Alluding to T. S. Eliot's allusion to *The Tempest*, Graham makes the metamorphoses of literary drowning ("pearled behind my eyes") into an analogy for the processes of self-change experienced in and through language use:

> So I spoke and died.
> So within the dead
> Of night and the dead
> Of all my life those
> Words died and awoke.

We speak and that moment of life dies and we are already other people, but the words, especially if they are printed, awake into a form of permanence. The deeper oddity of this metaphor, though, is that if poetic language is like the salt water of the sea, then poets on the job are simultaneously both in and out of their element – and if poetic language is one version of ordinary language use, then so are we all.

Graham's poetry began to appear during the Second World War, and, as in "Many without Elegy" or "Men Sign the Sea", among the first drownings that concern it are those of combatant sailors and flyers. This is not always evident in the early work because it is wedded to the widely noticed turn darkwards in the language of high modernism during the course of the 1930s – a turn led by writers with loyalties to the Celtic traditions in the British Isles. I'm thinking of Dylan Thomas's youthful fame, but more of *Finnegans Wake* (1939), a work that Graham clearly knew. He quotes from the "A hundred cares, a tithe of troubles and is there one who understands me?" passage at the book's close in "Notes on a Poetry of Release" (1946), and his correspondence is frequently imitative of its nonce and portmanteau words. The Apocalyptic movement in 1940s British poetry looks like a response to the acknowledged failure of the 1930s Oxford group to direct the course of events with a social activist plain style. Instead, taking a leaf from the Surrealist book, the Apocalyptic poets would tap into the obscure archetypes of a common unconscious so as to get back, behind the scenes, their access to a shared relevance which had been cut off through cultural division and global conflict on a directly-addressed level. There is, thus, much that is both heroic and quixotic about 1940s poetry in Britain and its aims and purposes could be more sympathetically understood. Yet the equally understandable post-war backlash from it, foreshadowed in Australia's Ern Malley Affair, seems to have left us in a perpetually reactive oscillation between ever more parodic versions of Joyce's Philip Drunk and Philip Sober.

The importance of W. S. Graham's later style is that it points to one possible way beyond that blocked oscillation. Criticism has tended to date his later style from *Malcolm Mooney's Land* (1971), but there are clear signs of it in poems such as "Since All my Steps Taken" and "Listen. Put on Morning" which open *The White Threshold* (1949) and it is fully formed in the "Three Letters" that conclude the volume. The "word-drunk" 1940s style was achieved by jamming together clusters of unusual adjective-noun pairings in long lines and capacious stanzas, as in "I am the frosty prophet of a grasshopping summer" – the last line of a final fifteen-line verse from "The Sixth Journey". The art of Dylan Thomas lay predominantly in his ability to sustain a strong rhythmic pulse through the heavy traffic of stressed syllables. Graham's early work has a less clear pulse; at times, as in "Explanation of a Map", its reading momentum can be clogged: "I cast, before peace grips my world's stoked womb, / High my bled ground". He alleviated this weakness, as here in "The Hill of Intrusion", by shortening his lines: "The ear sings better / Than any sound / It hears on earth / Or waters perfect". Shorter lines require far more concentration on unstressed monosyllables to maintain a rhythmic poise, and this simultaneously strengthens the auditory inevitability of the poetry by thinning out the adjectival traffic.

Graham had been concerned with the poet's cultural isolation from the beginning. His great insight was that this theme could be given an acute focus by locating it in the problems of specific, intimate exchanges. Once again this starts much earlier than is assumed by the superficial divide of the publishing gap between his 1955 and 1971 volumes. It has been clearly located by the time of the "Three Letters" of 1948, dedicated to his recently dead mother, and the series of "Letters" that follow "The Nightfishing" itself. What this produces is poetry whose themes are recognizably those of mid-century high modernism. Illuminating comparisons can be made with issues of isolation and communication in the theatre of Samuel Beckett and of Harold Pinter – one of Graham's long-term sustainers. The intimacy of address in these and later poems to his parents, artist friends, and, above all, to his wife, make his work more profoundly communal than is assumed in superficial comparisons with the much-advertised poetic responsibility of 1950s social realism.

Yet Graham's achievement came at quite a high price. He may not have been on the archangelic level of Coleridge, but he did subscribe to a romantic theory of art and damage. In an unused section from "The Dark Dialogues" published in *Aimed at Nobody*, we can read:

> I hope I do not write
> Only for those few
> Others like myself
> Poets maimed for the job.

Fairly inert syllabics, these; and they do no more than voice the reasonable fear that he is too much of a poet's poet. He needn't have worried, though. It's practically a definition of a good poet that she or he is, and will survive the reputation of being, a poet's poet. Margaret Blackwood and Robin Skelton, the editors of *Aimed at Nobody*, provided this poem with a title in square brackets. The poems from this collection with titles that are Graham's own tend to be of a higher quality with a greater degree of finish. The poet liked this "maimed for the job" idea enough to repeat it in correspondence. He may have decided to let that bit of poetry stay unpublished in his lifetime because the phrase had found a far more definitive and moving formulation in "The Thermal Stair", an elegy for the painter Peter Lanyon who had died in a 1964 gliding accident:

> The poet or painter steers his life to maim
>
> Himself somehow for the job. His job is Love
> Imagined into words or paint to make
> An object that will stand and will not move.

But like the problem of whether it can be martyrdom and not merely suicide if heretical believers put themselves in the way of persecution, there must be an issue about the exact situations in which an artist "steers his life to maim / Himself". Graham's line ending leaves momentarily open the possibility that it won't be only "Himself" that is getting maimed in life. There's a lesson to be learnt from the way in which Joyce himself, researching the themes of *Exiles* and *Ulysses*, encouraged the platonic enthusiasm of Roberto Prezioso for Nora Barnacle in 1912–13, stimulating his own jealousy to the extent of publicly humiliating Prezioso. Graham's letters and poems to the painter Roger Hilton reveal him intimately involved with both self-inflicted and collateral damage, while distinctly robust in his awareness of how it needs to be fended off and creatively survived: "All this virile anger and destruction. Why not somehow say it through your paintings"; or "Why don't you try to … make yourself paint from 8 in the morning to 12 midday. Something must be superimposed on the illness of being alive."

You could, though, suspect Graham of putting a brave front on a maimed life with the measure of control and aim in that word "steer". Maybe the romantic creator just messes up his life and then claims that it was all planned so as to produce "love" in "art". Yeats may write that "The intellect of man is forced to choose / Perfection of the life, or of the work", so as to lament consequences of the choice made. Yet there is no such dilemma. You can't guarantee that you will get the one by neglecting the other, and you may well muck up your life anyway by thinking in such crudely contrasted terms. This is one of the reasons why Henry James's story "The Lesson of the Master" could be advising us not to take guidance about how to live from people who recommend we devote ourselves solely to art. Yet even James, in this story, appears to entertain the flattering and possibly deluded notion that such devotion will bring the rewards that "compromising" by also living a life will deny. But that way sadness lies.

Another of the divide-and-rule conceptual traps in contemporary culture is that separating the sheep of supposedly private relations between poets and readers, from the goats of projected public roles for writers intervening in public debates at moments of national and international crisis. The latter of these, curiously congruent with 1950s ideas of poetic responsibility, has been claimed for vanguard writing which might take as its model a Milton or Mayakovsky (both painfully defeated, as it happens, in their public careers). The former, the private poet, is then marginalized as socially quietistic. Again, though, Graham's work shows how false this dichotomy may be. "Notes on a Poetry of Release" is focused on the intimate action of poetry in its placement between writer and reader: "The poem is not a handing out of the same packet to everyone, as it is not a thrown-down heap of words for us to choose the bonniest. The poem is the replying chord to the reader. It is the reader's involuntary reply." Or again: "The meaning of a poem is itself, not less a comma. But then to each man it comes into new life. It is brought to life by the reader and takes part in the reader's change." As Rilke put it in "Archäischer Torso Apollos", "Du Mußt dein Leben ändern" (You must change your life); and the fourth of Roy Fisher's "Handsworth Liberties" concludes that "in the crowd of exchanges / we can change". In poetry, as in everything else, the public and the private are neither distinct nor separable cultural spaces. "About the Stuff", an *Aimed at Nobody* poem from 1968, addresses itself to the "lens of language" with which a boy might go out to start a fire in summer, but

> Who wants to set the whole hill-side
> Bracken foxgloves and playing vixens
> On fire? No, only it is I want
> To disturb the paper, to burn a sense
> Of a changed other person in
> On to the white of this public skin.

We can hear Graham working to effect that change in the discovered rhyme of "vixens" and "sense", or in the stressing of the preposition "in" at a line-ending, one of three such parts of speech in a row, so as to effect the stanza's close. That local torque applied to spoken talk's stress-patterns is what the poet does to "burn a sense / Of a changed other person". W. S. Graham's 1946 manifesto concludes by inviting us to "endure the sudden affection of the language." We should take him at his word.

Reviews

The same war continues

Denise Levertov, *New Selected Poems,* edited by Paul A. Lacey,
with a preface by Robert Creeley, Bloodaxe, £9.95, ISBN 1852246577

Denise Levertov has sometimes been regarded as a minor poet, categorised according to the male poets who influenced her – Eliot is audible in her early work, and later she engaged collaboratively with Williams. She once wrote that "I had, without my noticing it or understanding what it meant, been chosen, tacitly, by some groups of male poets, or by individuals, as the exception that proved the rule – the rule that poetry was a masculine prerogative and that women were, by and large, either Muses or servants." But her development from an Objectivist faith in poetic perception through Christian devotion suggests a unique poetic destiny. Despite its eccentric typesetting and lack of notes (other than those provided by Levertov herself for her late books), this *New Selected Poems* offers a useful sample of these transformations.

Levertov alerts readers to her position within networks of male writers, most explicitly when she rebuts Jack Spicer's misogynist reading at Mill Valley in her poem "Hypocrite Women". But her idea of femininity was not confrontational. Rather, in poems such as "In Mind" and "The Women" it is arranged as a binary opposition between the homespun nurturer and the ragged, raging moon-goddess. Levertov often describes personhood as a contest between such contraries. This contest is probably a legacy of her religious upbringing, and the imperative to repress her body's impulses; she writes of her mother, "It had not been given her / to know the flesh as good in itself". But even within religious discipline the body could be celebrated for its powers of perception, which break down the opposition between self and world: "with how much gazing", she continues, her mother's "life has paid tribute to the world's body!" Levertov wrote intoxicated poems about sexual desire, and her background as a dancer suggests itself in her attentiveness to the physical and the gestural. But the opposition between grace and sinfulness, the self and others, is present even in her moving elegiac "Olga Poems" where her sister is her opposite, fierce, dark-eyed, ultimately "unknowable". Such oppositions seem integral to the patterns of her poetic thought.

Many of Levertov's poems, especially after her divorce, describe feelings of loneliness and isolation which came to be satisfied through the companionship of God. "Solitude within multitude seduced me early", she wrote, and Robert Creeley, in his preface, speculates that her conversion to Catholicism was motivated by a desire "to come into a company, a gathering of all, a determined yielding of such distinction and isolating privilege". That conversion was also a commitment to hope amidst the ravages of war. Her life started and ended with war; Levertov served as a nurse during the Blitz, and died in 1997 after the Gulf War. "The same war // continues. / We have breathed the grits of it in, all our lives". Deeply involved with the anti-war movement (she visited North Vietnam in 1972), she questioned the validity of her poetic vocation in such dark times. Her hope for poetry as a model of right thinking focuses on its ability to transform simple acts of perception into moments of transcendental clarity. Her poems celebrate "what's not found / at once, but lies // within something of another nature, / in repose, distinct". That act of discovery – distinct from the imposition of language on nature through metaphor – was also a feature of what she called her poetry's "organic form".

For Levertov the transformative power of imagination offers hope to human society, and imitates divine creativity. In "Mass for the Day of St. Thomas Didymus", she praises the divine as Imagination, which "wrought" powers and principalities in order "to give / to the Vast Loneliness / a hearth, a locus". Similarly, "Making Peace" hears poets commanded to "give us / imagination of peace, to oust the intense, familiar / imagination of disaster". But peace cannot be conjured from the imagination, she writes, any more than a poem can be imagined before it is made: "A feeling towards it, / dimly sensing a rhythm, is all we have / until we begin to utter its metaphors, / learning them as we speak".

Humans often seem unwilling to learn. "Life at War" worries over "delicate Man, whose flesh / responds to a caress, whose eyes / are flowers that perceive the stars", but who can turn away in silent disregard from genocide in Vietnam. Though in her prose Levertov endorses revolutionary politics, the idealism of her poetic representations of "Man" produces another irresolvable contrary. Her poems consequently veer between highly aestheticized descriptions of natural objects and landscapes and the most violent imagery thrown up by contemporary news.

Levertov's late poems nonetheless express the hope that "We have only begun to know / the power that is in us if we would join / our solitudes in the communion of struggle". She especially identified with the doubting St Thomas, and accounts for her spiritual awakening as a moment when she "entered the unhealed wound", and suddenly felt "light, light streaming / into me, over me, filling the room". This experience recalls her description of poetic inspiration in an interview in *The Minnesota Review*: "What happens is a withdrawal, by the imagination, from that first act of attention to the events. The head of the imagination is drawn back like the head of a snake about to strike. There is a silent explosion, and a blue light fills the room." As her poetry becomes a testament of faith, however, it loses the formal and prosodic clarity which shone in the earlier work. She asks "When you discover / your new work travels the ground you had traversed / decades ago, you wonder, panicked, / 'Have I outlived my vocation?'", but reassures herself that knowledge is cyclical, recurrent. She renews the old questions with new, Catholic wonder. In the late poems her grasping after refined prosody and simple correspondence between word and thing has been replaced with a conviction which, though never settled, is finally "in repose, distinct".

ANDREA BRADY

Nor any drop to drink

Michael Longley, *Snow Water*, Cape, £8, ISBN 0224072579
Matthew Hollis, *Ground Water*, Bloodaxe, £7.95, ISBN 85224657X
Mario Petrucci, *Heavy Water*, Enitharmon, £8.95, ISBN 1900564343

Snow water is pure water from melted snow, apparently prized in Japan for making tea: its seeming blandness, undoubted clarity, symbolic calm, and stimulus to fine aesthetic distinctions together make it an appropriate emblem for Michael Longley's eleventh book of verse. Unified in tone almost to a fault, the collection splits up neatly according to subject, with groups of poems about birds, about Italy, and about wars (the Great War, the Trojan War, the Troubles); the largest group describes the land- and water-scape in and around Carrigskeewaun, County Mayo. (The place-name alone pops up ten times in nine poems.) Longley writes (has long written) a poetry of watercolours and woodwinds, of carved and sanded lines marked "handle with care". Take the love lyric "Arrival":

> It is as though David had whitewashed the cottage
> And the gateposts in the distance for this moment,
> The whooper swans' arrival, with you wide awake
> In your white nightdress at the erratic boulder
> Counting through binoculars. Oh, what day is it
> This October? And how many of them are there?

Notice the neat shifts from subjunctive ("as though") to actual ("you ... in your white nightdress"), from past to present to the future, the unknown; notice the joke about Yeats's "Wild Swans at Coole". Notice, also, Longley's deft hexameters (doubtless drawn from his training in classics), which few other poets writing in English can manage now. Those lengthy lines (especially when they're hexameters), with their characteristically sinuous syntax, make it impossible for the poems to shout or denounce, easy for them to confide, invite, whisper, cherish (or mumble).

At the end of *The Mayor of Casterbridge*, Thomas Hardy's heroine resolves to pursue "the cunning enlargement, by a species of microscopic treatment, of those minute forms of satisfaction that offer themselves to everybody not in positive pain; which, thus handled, have much of the same inspiring effect upon life as wider interests cursorily embraced". Longley seems to have made the same resolution. Everything in any of his domestic or rural settings can become, as Longley puts it, "part of the composition" – stuffed birds, "cooking smells", "Oriental" sketches, a smithy, "pheasants' heather stands", miners, conversations in doorways. (Longley's subgenres are less like other poets' subgenres than like those of nineteenth-century painters.) His humility, his way with the ancient world, and his painterly love for domestic detail join hands in perhaps my favourite of his new poems, a defence of the ancient Greek poet Praxilla, whose name survives because (male) authors mocked her:

> Praxilla was *not* 'feeble-minded' to have Adonis
> Answer that questionnaire in the underworld:
> 'Sunlight's the most beautiful thing I leave behind,
> Then the shimmering stars and the moon's face,
> Also ripe cucumbers and apples and pears.'
> She is helping me unpack these plastic bags.
> I subsist on fragments and improvisations.
> Lysippus made a bronze statue of Praxilla
> Who 'said nothing worthwhile in her poetry'
> And set her groceries alongside the sun and moon.

The collection's other deft technical triumphs include an unmistakably comic zeugma and a serious one-line elegy: "my lost lamb lovelier than all the wool". Longley errs, when he errs, on the side of insignificance, rather than that of unearned significance; he would rather end up unimportant than sound self-important. As with his acknowledged model Edward Thomas, those preferences let the work as a whole appeal even when individual poems do seem flimsy or slight: who needs Power, when you can have Delight?

Matthew Hollis's debut, *Ground Water*, offers aural assurance, lyric sincerity, and undoubted consistency – its chief symbols are rain, floods, shorelines, rivers, storms, fishing, and ploughing; its chief topics lovers and ex-lovers, deceased relatives, and Irish and English locales; its chief influences

Heaney, Muldoon, Longley, cummings, Heaney, Heaney and Heaney. "Wintering" (the first poem) remembers Hollis's father as a Heaneyesque rural ghost: "if I listen, I can hear him out / in the kitchen, scudding potatoes". "The Orchard Underwater" follows choughs "inking the air with trial after trial, / localised as downpour, a pencil of rain". (See Heaney's "The Rain-Stick"; then see the end of *Station Island*.) "Passing Place" replicates both the scansion and the tone of Heaney's poems about Irish place names, seeking "the good words / which lay // just under the tongue", "the mor / and mull / of the language", "the loam of ourselves / tilled over, / grown in". Hollis's otherwise attractive sequence "One Man Went to Mow" gives us a farm implement the poet inherited from his father, and a cadence inherited from Heaney's "Alphabets":

> Not yet old enough to span the handle
> I'd run the gat and burn of the riverbank,
> the traps for knapped rabbits; my father closing
> the cloth on his sickle, petal by wintering petal.

Hollis's broader interests hew closely to Heaney's: slippery memory and self-doubting nostalgia; the drive to speak for humble rural ancestors, whose hard physical labour grounds or resembles the honest making of poems; devotion to rare one- and two-syllable nouns and verbs ("jounce," "sill-lines," "cloughs," "karren," "welter and coup"); flickering transcendence which the poet encourages himself to trust. (Heaney tells himself to "walk on air against your better judgment"; Hollis hopes to "open the door / and step out on the might-be of water.") Some of the least Heaneyish poems have clear models elsewhere. (Hollis: "not even the leaves / can lay down with such gentleness"; cummings: "not even the rain has such small hands.") The problem is not that Hollis has taken so much from Heaney, or from anyone, but that he has not done enough with what he took: if, as Eliot wrote, immature poets borrow, mature poets steal, then Hollis seems obviously immature.

He also seems, in the strictest sense, promising. When he does not sound just like Heaney he can sound impressive, with a gift for lyrical similes. One of the rural elegies, a poem about waking at midnight called "Winter Break", ends "like snowmen getting up to go, / whose love is cold, whose love not cold enough". "Sandwriting" ends beautifully "as one by one the oil lamps wicked across the bay / like a hundred homes standing up to be counted". He also has a neat trick of turning raptly descriptive love poems into breakup poems near their endings, as in "Skin Contact", a tender and subtle aubade.

If *Snow Water* aspires to air small pleasures, Mario Pretucci's *Heavy Water* is weighty and painful instead, The book-length sequence describes (most of its poems are spoken by) victims and witnesses to the nuclear disaster which began at Chernobyl in 1986, and which still blights swaths of Ukraine and Belarus. Some of the words, and apparently all of the characters, derive (as Petrucci's prologue explains) from a searing collection of oral histories, *Voices from Chernobyl* (1999), compiled by Svetlana Alexievich, and translated by Antonina Bouis. *Voices* reads like a Mass Observation study of Hell. So, sometimes, do Petrucci's poems. Victims of gamma-ray poisoning die over days and weeks, irradiating everyone and everything near: a nurse tells the wife of a firefighter, "Each time you hold his hand is a year off your life". Evidence of Soviet corruption (if not of our corrupt hearts, of original sin), Chernobyl unarguably saw nature corrupted, remaking gardens, bees, weddings, eggs, as discoloured masks, either sterile white or ash-black: "sitting in a chair / in an empty house", one refugee views "a black calf / with hair to the ground. It was // eating stones. Its black eyes shone". A Marian chapel in the contaminated zone stands for failed salvation of all kinds, "the faint caesium glow // of her cape" lighting a "face white / with lead":

> Now
> old ones say – *See her*
> *and die*. All who kneel
> here know. She too
>
> once held a child
> that would not cry.

These characters' exceptional testimonies point up a general fate – we all die; we all plan, or fail to plan, for our own deaths; we all try to figure out how close we can get to one another without harming the people we love. If the book thus becomes a *memento mori*, it also offers a public warning: its evidence of continued contamination, its laments for the walking dead, accrete a sense of disaster, of collapse on every level (ecological, familiar, personal) which most people in wealthy nations (9/11 notwithstanding) have not known, and may know soon. (Even before "dirty bomb" was a commonplace term, Alexievich warned that editing her oral history gave her "the feeling that I was recording the future".)

Like James Fenton's *Children in Exile* and Carolyn Forché's *The Country Between Us*, *Heavy Water* competes not only with other poetry, but with historians' and journalists' prose, and with survivors' testimony (which, in this case, the poems continually quote). To his already powerful material, Petrucci can add well-managed mimetic effects: assigned to bury a still-hot reactor, "Even the robots refuse. Down tools. Jerk up / their blocked heads, shiver in invisible hail". Often, though, Petrucci's line shapes seem arbitrary, his diction unexceptional; many of his unrhymed couplets might as well be (moving, concise) prose. If a poem about pinball or field mice affects us deeply, the reason (unless we are pinball wizards or mouse fanciers) probably lies in the poet's treatment. By contrast, a poem like Petrucci's need not be especially accomplished, nor original, in its forms and sounds in order for its matter to stick in our minds: it need only be good enough. *Heavy Water* is good enough.

STEPHEN BURT

Choreography, of course

Lee Harwood, *Collected Poems*, Shearsman Books, ISBN 090756240X

On page 243, approximately the middle of Lee Harwood's 522 page *Collected Poems*, is "London To Brighton":

> on the late night train home
>
> "kind gentle creature he was, died quite young"
> heard from the next seat down
> "quite diffident, and nervous"
>
> "I shall have to answer at the Pearly Gates.
> He declared a passionate love to me,
> And . . ." (the rest unheard – train noise)
>
> now all that comes through
> is noise of talk and small laughter,
> but none coming through clear
>
> "choreographer" (of course(?))
>
> In love with the man in one's life
> or not, as the case may be

Lee Harwood loves to tell stories, but he likes them with interruptions, holes for the imagination to fill, twists and turns as if the story makes itself up as it goes along. Choreographer? Of course. He uses prose to achieve some of his effects, quotes like a collagist, loves the article "the", pauses to note the actual world and moves on. Perhaps the most cosmopolitan English poet of his generation, Harwood has gone far from Brighton, his home for over thirty years: to Paris, Greece, New York City, Boston, the American West and the mountains of Wales. Cosmopolitan, too, in his openness to the teachings of Pound, Tristan Tzara (he has translated his poems), Jorge Luis Borges, John Ashbery and Constantine Cavafy. As this book proceeds, Borges's influence becomes evident, as does the "amused tenderness" Harwood finds in Cavafy. Pound's instruction can be seen in the primacy of image. What Harwood drew from Ashbery is not so easy to discern. Most poets influenced by Ashbery (I'm thinking of American poets) were besotted and emerged looking like clones. Few have been as adept as Harwood at learning from and resisting Ashbery.

Harwood's interest in story, the broken-off tale reentered, descends in part from Ashbery's scattering bits of *Beryl and the Bi-plane* through his radical, exhilarating early poem "Europe". Harwood may well have recognized his own predilection for collage and suspended narrative in Ashbery's poem. And there is something else; something harder to define, that Harwood may have absorbed through Ashbery. While Harwood is unafraid of emotion, and over the course of his writing has come to embrace frank statements of his feelings, he is a quiet poet. Ashbery too is quiet, and his poems take their time unfolding. In both poets the reader is allowed his distance. Perhaps the best way to put this is that both poets are confident enough to let the reader do what he will with their poems. Certainly the reader of "London To Brighton" has Harwood's permission to take the poem "as the case may be".

This emphasis on Harwood's touchstone poets is necessary for two reasons. He is a difficult poet to quote and a list of his best poems would be misleading. For all the freestanding poems in this book, Harwood is not a poet of best poems, but of poems that flow together – the book abounds in sequences – so that Harwood's work is a river not a series of isolate ponds. In effect you can start anywhere in this book and you'll soon know if Harwood is your cup of tea or not. In this regard his work is similar to that of Tom Raworth, England's other cosmopolitan poet of the post-*New American Poetry* generation.

On the other hand, Harwood's work could not be more different from that of Kingsley Amis and Philip Larkin. This will be obvious at once, but is worth amplifying. For this American reader, Larkin's spareness has appeal and his poems can be powerfully terse. It is their sharply defined limits, their insistence on gloom and the enormous "no" in their soul that will not sustain. Many accept this strong medicine as vision, but seen from the vantage of Harwood's book Larkin's way seems a willed refusal. To do what? To go, in

Harwood's words, "into the unknown or barely guessed at. It's in the reader's hands". If Larkin is a refuser, Harwood is an accepter, a poet who seeks and finds poems in the flow of language and life.

The reason to read this book, and the pleasure you will take in doing so, comes down to Harwood's tender regard for the things and people of this world. There is a great, in-drawing, open-heartedness in his poetry that carries the reader along. This is not a matter of statement. For all Harwood's clarity he avoids the big statement. It is a matter, rather, of regard, in all the senses of that word: to look attentively, to hold in esteem, to be careful in thought or attention. Quiet virtues, yes, but no less vital and worthy for that. Over the forty years of work tracked in this book, these virtues shine.

WILLIAM CORBETT

Under the counter

Ed Dorn, *Chemo Sábe*, Limberlost Press, $20, ISBN 0931659701

Ed Dorn's was no cosy vision of humanity, but often an abrupt and indignant striving after sincerity of perception. Even so, *Chemo Sábe* contains poems that he could hardly have wished to write. For they represent that handful written between his diagnosis with pancreatic cancer in 1997 and his death in 1999, when he was contending not just with the grim vortices of contemporary America, but with the grimmer recognition that it wouldn't be for much longer.

Dorn is here besieged from a multitude of directions: by the toxicity of modern consumer culture – the shoppers emerging from Cub Food "like overweight ants dragging their take / away from an abandoned sandwich"; by his own cells which "demand evermore progeny and evermore food"; and by the armoury of drugs brought in to reduce them. These idols of the chemo, Benadryl, Decadron and Taxol, are the instruments of torture which, as with Samuel Johnson, are to keep the poet alive from hour to hour. But they are also names to conjure with:

> The wind twirls in
> The aeolian Colorado dust
> The hand with the Atavan,
> The keeper of the exit
> Oxycontin could put the dead to sleep
>
> ("Denver Dawn: with Ceiling Fan")

In these lines, "Ode to the West Wind" juts into *High Plains Drifter*, while the Mayan Book of the Dead is engraved on the counter at Rite Aid. It's a characteristically masterful superimposition which courts incongruity but avoids mere pastiche. Dorn was not ultimately a postmodernist. Rather his eye glided surely over life's most erratic traits and folded them into singular acts of perception. Only someone who could habitually shoot round corners could have devised an exam question for his students at Essex University along the lines of: "What connections are there between Whitman's poetics and General Westmoreland's military strategy in Vietnam?".

At times Dorn's love of succinctness twins with sheer gall in a kind of bullet-point doggerel – "Throat ripping / Ball torching / Fire balling" is his Coke-ad inspired response to the effects of iodine. Another kind of succinctness emerges in the following complete poem: "Will pigs yet unborn / produce the enzymes booked / for the cells yet undivided?" *Chemo Sábe* is full of such artful reductions. In the 1980s Dorn's poetry became so acerbic and epigrammatic that it approached the formal purity of the bumper sticker. But another kind of clarity still reaches back to the cool bright lyricism he developed in the orbit of Black Mountain college in the 1950s: "Thin sheet-ice on Sloan's lake / 'dark white' shine, late February sun". Finally there's that sheer grace of diction in what were some of the last poetic lines he wrote: "Torn loose from / the human fabric, / adrift in the human breeze".

However, just as the panache and inventiveness of *Gunslinger*, Dorn's burlesque epic of the early 1970s, can obscure his other quieter – or more declamatory – voices, so the highlight of this book is "Chemo du Jour: The Impeachment on Decadron". It's a monster of a free verse ode which is equally a document from Dorn's cancer journal, a fantasy of political process and a shamanic ritual: Decadron sharpens the senses around the neocortex, enabling one to see "through walls and into / the present". As the drug inaugurates a holy war on the poet's stem cells, the day's news mushrooms in a grotesque hallucination over his brow – "I see W. J. Clinton / full humping St. Monicka" – which, for all its parodic excess, also hits home with a deadly accuracy. While Clinton avoids "coming" in one fraught arena, a compensatory experimental missile flames and launches from the carrier and, "as the nurse strips away the Medusan tubes of my oncology", it "arrives with punity / in the southern suburbs of Baghdad, ruined Cradle of Civilization". This was written in 1999. Only Dorn could hit that obscure angle at which hallucination, perception and political reportage intersect, forging a poem in which these minutes of a dying man become the terminal record of an aberrant culture. If this was intended for Bill, what poem would George have called forth – an oilman, and a Texan?

MATT FFYTCHE

Dismembered and remembered

Annemarie Austin, *Back from the Moon*, Bloodaxe, £7.95, ISBN 1852246235

Annemarie Austin's world is one of doubles and reflections. In *Back from the Moon*, as in previous collections, she is deeply engaged with shifting perspectives and changing perceptions. In "Haar", for example, the sea mist that envelopes the speaker is a "white chimney" distorting her vision; she sees "a ghost alsatian, big as a running horse" and "the pier on silver legs / reared up too high". Yet such distortions are only part of the picture:

> From the tower,
> he told me, he saw a different haar:
> folded over the headland like a shawl,
> smoking off the beach from a hundred campfires.

Such double-takes recur throughout the collection. Poems linked by a single image are frequently paired: "Haar" is followed by "Going West", in which the pier is taken as a starting-point; rivers and photographs and the act of painting are all rendered from different angles, and the comet for which the ear invents a sound in "Seen and Not Heard" is immediately followed by "a comet / like a diving bloom in the sky" in "The Train Now Leaving…". In the first short lyric it is the almost exclusive focus – the objective correlative for the bursting of the poet's eardrum. In the second poem it at first seems incidental, one of the many indicators that "something's not right". The poem instead appears dominated by swans: "afloat / in a field eating grass outside", flying "towards the train / a long time on great slow wings"; passing an orchard, even the light becomes "like a dismembered swan caught / in the sieve of branches". It is only in the final lines that the comet remakes the poem in its own image, as "the world outside writhes / in the comet's gaze, lets loose / its infestation of swans upon us". Even taken on its own, this poem shows the protean quality of Austin at her best, when the idea of "reflection" ceases to be explicitly her subject and instead manifests in a series of Escher-like transformations that render the physical world permeable. Yet the effect is further enhanced by its positioning, as each of the two comets is revisited and reinterpreted in the light of the other.

In the last part of the book doubling becomes a structural principle, with poems on the illness and memory loss of Austin's father answered by a sequence in which Austin imagines the mind's misperceptions and distortions from within. These are among the strongest poems in the collection. Austin is a natural story-teller and ventriloquist. In the first part of the book too she frequently assumes voices and situations: a nineteenth-century prince of Moncada; Cartier-Bresson and the anonymous subject of one of his photographs; a generic "Ageing Lady"; Claire Clairmont; Yeats after his death and burial. This, of course, is yet another way of altering familiar perspectives, yet in these earlier poems – despite some startling observations – it can on occasion seem slightly willed, or whimsical: a device for writing a poem rather than the inevitable voice of a poem that demanded to be written. In the poems on dementia, however, voice and compulsion come together. In one of the poems for her father, Austin describes the dismembering of a dead rabbit, and the appearance of a heron on a concrete island in the Barbican lake, disparate images which she can only relate by the direct address: "Daddy, this is really about you". But her despairing failure to formulate an adequate response is followed by the imaginative recreation of a state parallel to her father's condition. The last poem in the sequence for her father speaks directly of what her double will do, as hospital visitor, while her true self remains horror-struck outside. The answering sequence finds a way, through a shivered reflection, of re-opening the channels of communication.

JANE GRIFFITHS

STAND

QUARTERLY JOURNAL OF POETRY AND PROSE

FORTHCOMING ISSUES:
○ Short-Fiction Special (ed. Lorna Tracy)
○ Special in memory of Ken Smith

STILL AVAILABLE:
○ Translation
○ Geoffrey Hill Special
○ Leeds Poets
○ 50th Anniversary Issue

FOR SUBMISSIONS OR SUBSCRIPTIONS:

STAND@LEEDS.AC.UK
OR
STAND MAGAZINE
SCHOOL OF ENGLISH
UNIVERSITY OF LEEDS
LEEDS LS2 9JT

World of interiors

Robert Saxton, *Manganese*, £7.95, Oxford Poets, Carcanet, ISBN 1903039711

To place side by side the words "Oxford" and "poetry" releases – would anyone demur? – an unwelcome electricity. The term "Oxford Poets" which now graces a number of Carcanet books, including Robert Saxton's second collection, *Manganese*, fizzles and glows in a similar alarming manner. I don't know – does anyone?– what the phrase means (not, I think, exclusively poets living or working in Oxford and not, I think, exclusively poets from the old OUP list), but that electricity, like Robert Saxton's book, may tell us something interesting about the current state of British poetry. Of course the phrase gives us the shivers partly because the word "Oxford" conjures up all sorts of ideas – donnishness, inside-trackery, arrested development, public-school culture, what Auden called "private joking in a paneled room", in short, class – from which it would be nice to disassociate poetry. But I suspect the electricity also has something to do with one of the jagged (but let us hope, closing) fault-lines in British poetry between, on the one hand, academic culture, with its relative tolerance of experimental poetry and, on other hand, promotional culture, with its relative tolerance of populist poetry. Whichever way you cut it, "Oxford" is not a poetic word.

With the possible exception of Ted Hughes, the last English poet to close the fault-line between experimental poetry and its populist cousin was W. H. Auden. Auden could plausibly be caricatured as an Oxford poet, and as *Manganese* illustrates, his influence remains an enabling provocation, as well as a troubling reproof, to all subsequent English poets – and to "Oxford" poets in particular. That Saxton admires Uncle Wizz, and has learned a great deal from him, is obvious. Auden's signature is everywhere from the formal variety and the playfully camp diction to specific technical features; aphoristic cate-gorizations ("All cowboys long to torch their secret nest", "All saints become themselves by accident"), a Thirties-style use of the definite article ("the cancelled concert in the chestnut grove"), quadripartite lines with strange modifiers ("fierce janitors of unfashionable spas") and, as those janitors suggest, plentiful references to archaic and faintly dotty professions (ostlers, choirmasters, sandalmakers, gardeners, ringmasters).

But the influence extends well beyond these surface features. Because Auden's poetry, early and late, supplied the thrill of a peculiarly English form of Romantic interiority, alongside an even more thrilling critique of the same phenomenon, it has been difficult for those poets left admiring in his wake to retreat under their rugs. In one form or another, all poets influenced by Auden attempt to be "social". If the poet is genuinely "social" then this presents no problem. To propose an illustration for what I mean, if the poet is one who, to judge from their poetry, would not wish to be the last person left in the world (Ashbery, Wilbur, Paulin) then this aspect of Auden's influence will simply reinforce their deepest instincts. But if the poet is one – again, on the evidence of their poetry – who might well be happy left entirely alone in the world (Hill, Mahon, Plath) then this aspect of Auden's influence will cause severe critical feedback. Now it would be unfair to place Robert Saxton in this latter group but he is nearer to them than he is to the former. For one thing, the speakers of his poems often announce their desire for apartness ("Myself, I crave the cool sanctity of cinema") and the poems are saturated with images of privacy (in separate poems we find "a rabbit in its sand-cave" and "a dolphin trapped in a tide-cave"). As Sebastian Flyte playfully illustrates, the English version of Romantic interiority – consciousness purged of its threatening rivals – is especially welcoming to certain unthreatening rivals of consciousness including animals, children and, if Prince Charles is anything to go by, plants. Accordingly, Saxton's poetry includes numerous warm references to all of these. Animals in particular contribute to a characteristic temptation for the Oxford poet, the carefully textured den. For Saxton's poetry is full of interesting textures (no plastic-cups or breeze-blocks here, thank you) from chessboards, ivy and golems (remind you of anywhere?) to mink, eels and moths. His poems often move so as to dwell on, or come to rest in, an attractive visual texture ("A cherry tree's loose change / spilt in the sand …", "spangled with sand our shadowless dreams wear down to", "our hurricane a pillowfight").

The sonic upshot of this is a similar precoccupation with arresting aural textures, sometimes at the small expense of clarity. Saxton is fond of forms, like sestinas and villanelles, which use repeated words or lines, and he invents several similar forms of his own. One of his sestinas, "Safe Dreams" (the title is suggestive), shows how wonderfully his kind of interiority can work alongside these formal devices. Here is the opening stanza:

> Though you cover me safe
> with a hat, slice of sleep,
> the rain starts with my shoes.
> too late the sight of moths,
> holes like rain, another
> crime drifted beyond touch.

Indeed, Saxton likes these repeating end-words so much, his poem "Sleeping Rough" uses them all over again. Saxton's difficulty lies in turning, one would guess rather reluctantly, to the social world, and when such a turn occurs, there is often a jar in his otherwise splendid diction. Here is an example: "I'm bottomfishing in the gloom / Of the global share collapse – Dow warrior. / The heck if I can quite see what I'm doing." "Bottomfishing in the gloom" sounds marvelous – one senses the speaker would really like to retreat forever to such an underwater womblike fastness. But the balancing social commentary, such as it is, founders on that somewhat forced use of "The heck". The pattern is repeated throughout *Manganese*. The book's weakest poem is the last, a very contemporary social commentary dwelling in part on the marriage of Madonna and Guy Ritchie and in part on the speaker's desire to escape his parents, which altogether collapses in bathos. *Manganese* is a very enjoyable book to read, as subtle, various, ornamental and clever as Saxton's great mentor might have wished. But it remains to be seen if the socializing pull of the Audenesque will stifle the minor Mallarmé trying to get out:

> At last, a six-toed footprint,
>   melting, more gigantic still.
> The explorer sampling his aunt's cake,
>   bites upon a file.
> In the serpentine Great Wall
>   of the known world – a stile.

JOHN REDMOND

The blur of incandescent joy

Kate Clanchy, *Newborn*, Picador, £12.99, ISBN 0330419307

The poems in Kate Clanchy's *Newborn*, as both the title and cover photograph of a baby's head announce, trace the story of the coming of a baby, and the collection is blessed by the stars in the form of Emma Thompson: it reminds her of "that incandescent joy". The title is stretched to include the antics of a walking and talking infant under the term "newborn". This could be read as an ironic reference to the temporary nature of all things: almost as soon as a newborn merits the name it starts to shed it. In very occasional lines in the collection, there are small confirmations of such a reading, such as "The Dream of Warm Things", with the fearless lines

> I stroke the soft
> hot dome of his forehead, the furrow
> where the line will come.

In the opening poem, "One, Two", with "perhaps ten cells", Clanchy displays a typical precision:

> In the humid space beneath
> my dress, my body is bent
> in the small effort of buckling . . .

The poems move through the processes of pregnancy and childbirth. However, apart from the vivid "eager, even over-familiar / uncle-ish hard tweak at my waist" in "Pang", she also spares us much of the pain and the less pleasant aspects, and sentimentality often threatens. "The Other Woman", an apparent critique of the self-absorption of parenthood, teeters disturbingly on the edge of an indictment of childless women. Clanchy could learn from George Oppen's clear, tender, yet cold, "Sara In Her Father's Arms", which refers, like "One, Two", to the process of cell multiplication, or from her editor Don Paterson's "Waking with Russell" – a daring, impressive example of controlled use of emotional depth.

But there are shining moments too. "When You Cried", likening the baby to a salmon thrashing "like a choking fish", "searching upstream, / upstream, for the dark pool", carries echoes of Kahlil Gibran's wisdom:

> I thought
> you'd seen through us, that
> you knew this wasn't home.

The last lines of "Commonplace" catch the chatter of mother and child beautifully inside an image of the specifics of life and death:

> we walk
> on fields as green as any field,
> babbling like Falstaff when he died.

In her previous work, Clanchy has excelled in a sharp and bitter delicacy of touch, particularly in the taboo-breaking "Mitigation" in *Slattern*. Such a quality is still present here, but it never fills a whole poem, and often appears muted or blurred, as if half-edited out. This observation chimes with my recollection of a reading given by Clanchy two years ago, at the Commonwealth

Literature Festival in Manchester. Then, in her version of "In a Prospect of Flowers", a mother stands, proudly watching her child walk with his father. Her joy in him broadens, by the end of the poem, to include the scholarly father: "my scholar's gait". In the later *Newborn* version, the mother is walking with the father and son. Her intrusion into the scene strips that last phrase of its broadening generosity, for the speaker now also celebrates herself: "our scholars' gait". Perhaps the difficulties I find with *Newborn* lie in Clanchy's determination to follow a similar route, editing too much of herself in?

JUDY KENDALL

Laments and messages

Frank McGuinness, *The Stone Jug*, Gallery, £8.95, ISBN 185235352X

Frank McGuinness once said in an interview that paintings were possibly more important to him as a source of inspiration than literature. It's true that the language of the plays which have made his name – *Observe the Sons of Ulster Marching towards the Somme*, *Someone Who'll Watch Over Me* – is strongly visual. Similarly, the poems that work best in *The Stone Jug* seem to result from a painter's eye for colour and symbol. These underpin his major themes of exile, identity, and homosexuality.

The opening poem, "Fahan Hill", is set in Buncrana, Donegal (McGuinness's home town) and uses many images that recur throughout the book. Red is for suffering – "Crown of thorn / those red days" – and becomes the dominant colour. And religious imagery is never far away, no sooner mentioned than angrily rejected: "Sorrow is the way of the saints. Sinner, / I will spit on the rod".

This juxtaposition of abstract opposites – saint/sinner – recurs throughout "Gyrfalcon", a sixty sonnet sequence addressed mostly by a man to his unobtainable male lover. Hell follows heaven, rich is balanced by poor, truth by a lie, a marriage is both loss and gain – the sequence has its roots in the form's tradition of paradox. Some work better than others. "Roar" is skilfully done:

> Still, I continue to write to you. Lost,
> alone, fearing being alone and lost,
> what started out as a way of saving
> myself, damning myself, treacherous, know

this above all else, I always say no,
I'm in the business of losing, saving.

The gyrfalcon's habitat is the Northern Antarctic – the title was inspired by a rare sighting of the bird in West Clare – and the sonnets are partly about wishing to introduce a foreigner/lover to aspects of Ireland. Anger is the dominant emotion when grappling with religion: "Worship the god who loves murder and drunkard. / That's what I offer to strangers I love. / This country for you . . .". Religious figures, too, get used mercilessly: "leaves / are covering the place in their soft brown / habit of monks kicked from summer convents".

At times, though, the repetition of abstracts, combined with the recurring images (angels, demons, leaves, birds), makes you feel like you are listening to a sestina in an echo chamber. And the final couplets often show the strain of the relentless end rhyme: "These poems are lies. I need you like rain. / Meeting you, I could never be the same".

That's not the case with the poems in the third part of *The Stone Jug*. "The Wife's Lament" is loosely based on an Old English lyric from the Exeter Book. Here, McGuinness adopts the voice of a woman who has married a king in order to bring an end to a feud and finds herself abandoned. "I bought / my freedom once, a gown of golden fishskin / torn from my husband's back", she says. She has witnessed and perhaps done terrible things, but like the original lyric, the narrative remains opaque.

"The Husband's Message" that follows is spoken by a soldier (the narrator of the Old English poem is either a messenger or a stick carved with a message). This soldier, though, is not relating a plea for a deserted wife to join her husband, as is thought to be the case in the original. Instead, he is reporting on a feud:

> In this country people live apart. Their choice.
> They set fire to themselves and their neighbours.
> They'll drive to death in a golden Rolls Royce

These are chilling narratives. It's tempting to conclude that it's the skill of McGuinness the playwright that takes off here, leaving the poet behind. At the very least, they send you back to the elusive, riddle-like, tenth-century originals.

JANET PHILLIPS

Flying home from Budapest

Michael Murphy, *Elsewhere*, Shoestring Press, £7.95, ISBN 1899549870

"Elsewhere" is a place Michael Murphy is always trying to reach, an elusive world where memory and death intersect, "neither here nor there". If elsewhere is the realm of the past, however, it's also that of the future: the future that might have been but never was. It's "a lifetime away" from the present, forever out of reach, the kind of place where an ex-lover "rehearses what it is / she never said and didn't mean" ("Vertigo"). Elsewhere is, by definition, wherever Murphy isn't, so how is he supposed to get there? This paradoxical longing colours much of Murphy's first collection, from a series of elegies for his late mother to the title piece, a childhood vignette about finding a dead thrush in the snow. He buries it among the "bulbs / sprouting in the loamy darkness / under [the] shed". Then he keeps an eerie vigil, waiting "to see if – if – feathers, beak and all the / intricately coiled stuff // had, with morning, ascended".

The parallels between the bulbs and the small bird's body – both containing intricately coiled matter – tempt us to imagine the thrush sprouting back to life, ascending from the soil reborn. Yet even as Murphy dangles the possibility of miracle before us, he offers its exact opposite. Death is inescapable; what will ascend is only the thrush's ghost, rising into the afterlife. At first glance similar, bulbs and bird are in reality irredeemably different: vegetable vs. animal, life vs. death. Murphy packs such dualities and ironies – his own intricately coiled stuff – into the twelve lines of the poem with stunning ingenuity and delicacy.

Other pieces, though less successful, likewise explore the natural world and its contradictions, the "promise of return" embodied by a pomegranate seed in winter, or the way a hyacinth bulb is "a stoppered glass / the sun will break" come spring. Growth requires breakage – "cells split / and open" – as becomes clear in "The Garden", in which Murphy hacks away at the earth. "I have in mind the burying of things", he begins ominously; but instead of burying the dead, he ends by planting seeds, facilitating new life. In "Thrush" he watches a bird smash open a mollusc and devour it, a scene at once grisly and commonplace: death feeding growth.

Murphy returns to the themes of memory and distance, of elsewhereness, in the sequence "Postcards From Budapest". Something in him is irresistibly drawn to reminiscence, the "glassy kiss" of the past. If nostalgia often lapses into self-indulgence (as he admits: "It's tempting to get maudlin"), he's equally capable of engineering luminous images that evoke the here and now. Mortality may beckon – "time is measured" – yet on one afternoon, just for an instant, "the river / fires the city's windows, light builds light", and the "[s]hadows steady / on their coltish legs". The sun's movement, though it signifies the passing of time, also calls this beautiful moment into existence, one in which we can "look up ... and trust ourselves alive".

A worrying number of poems in *Elsewhere* fail to reach such heights, like Murphy's sugary paeans to his partner and baby, or the jarringly jaunty, pun-filled fable of "The Fox and the Crow". Hopefully he'll continue more in the vein of "47° 28' N, 19° 1' E", an account of flying home from Budapest in which each line ("The air we breathe has been breathed before") simultane-ously applies to the physical experience of plane travel, the concept of home, and the quality of memory. All three share "a silence / touched from the wires of a shallow box: / a kind of harmony ... / charged with music like hushed bells". At their best, Murphy's complex, multivalent poems ring with the same sort of harmony.

JANE YEH

❧

All lines are busy

Andrea Brady, *Cold Calling*, Barque Press (www.barquepress.com),
£4, ISBN 1903488338

"Cold Calling" has an obvious reference: the practice of telephoning unannounced in the hope of making a sale. But "calling" could also be taken to mean a vocation, a bardic responsibility; "cold", as in "cold-shouldered" or "cold reception", might imply a sense of the shunned, the misprised, the ignored. Together, the words coalesce into a particular vision of poetic duty and its potential problems. Halfway through this genuinely remarkable, desperately important pamphlet, I started to think I'd heard the title beforehand, until I realised I was mis-remembering the opening of T. S. Eliot's "The Magi" – "A cold coming we had of it". But Eliot's poem still seemed significant, with its sense of hardship and possible epiphany, even its Middle East setting. By the time that readers reach the title poem, significantly placed at the end of the collection, they are accustomed to the political resonances and sly layerings of Brady's poetry, and attuned to the image of the call-centre workers and their voices "twitching like free peoples", at the same time as the anonymity of the transaction conjures catching the common cold ("but are the cheeks bacchic / or tropic illness"). With urgency and complexity, Brady creates a profoundly rich, activated poetry. She is anything but commonplace.

She employs techniques and aspects of style that might remind you of Gertrude Stein (unexpected stammers and break-neck switches), or of Veronica Forrest-Thomson (an equally unexpected lyricism). Where Brady seems radically different is in the ends to which these devices are used. Despite the allusive and elusive qualities, this is a poetry operating in a fundamentally public sphere. There are moments of collage, when she infects banal phrases with a wry turn ("is that dream available in time for Christmas"); and similarly, she finds in decontextualised segments a gleam of extra importance or actual beauty ("life sentences running consecutively").

If, on picking up this collection, you are startled, or even bemused, by the richness of the textures, or the inter-cutting of the registers, start with what Brady says about language itself. In "Cellular Contact" she places two anchors: "Language isn't bad enough yet" and "Anything you might say is legislated" (not to mention the glorious, double-take line-break in "Keep going until hate demolishes the concrete // poem and gives us all the lie"). Brady's language is co-opted from her by manifestations of abusive power; political, military, bureaucratic, consumerist and sexual colonisation of the words we use demands their recapture. But not by force: by stealth. There are buried puns (the "newter" language she wants), as well as outrageous flourishes ("dresses mutton as lamb // to satisfy Wolfowitz despite Colin's clout"). These are guerrilla tactics against a homogenising spin that denies words their abundance. How can you testify to horror in the tones of the perpetrator? Where does compromising begin? These are questions that Paul Celan struggled with after the events of the Second World War – the fact that Buchenwald now had a double meaning – and that Brady faces uncompromisingly. W. S. Graham famously asked "What is the language using us for?", but his language was an almost transcendental entity. Brady rephrases this sentence: the poet is "used" by language in a far more sinister, spent manner.

This should not imply that "Cold Calling" offers a thesis on linguistics rather than poems of exquisite polish. With such daring collocations as "webs placed / in the old days now strong / as marriaging steel", and dark, seething ironies, as in "the right to life is more than / abortion shrapnel, a Row joke. / The best states are not of the mind", Brady proves she can unite instant impact with haunting persistence.

The ongoing, deepening war in Iraq provides a context for some of these poems, but not all: nor would it be fair to categorise this book as being an erudite form of protest. The global and the local are always concatenated. All these poems have narratives – not just a story – and they have speakers – not just a voice. But the quality of their emotional substance is for each and every individual reader to construct: it does not hector, or inveigle; it resists telling you what to think. In, for example, the wonderful "torn" poem "Summa", the reader is automatically forced to decide: left hand poem, right hand poem, or the combination of both? A review of *Cold Calling* cannot "provide a key", since the poetry itself courageously opposes the reductive and debilitating use of language. Brady presents no uncomplicated issues; and the bravery of that stance is matched only by the sheer bravura of her work.

STUART KELLY

Malachite and pearls

Sue Hubbard, *Ghost Station*, Salt, £8.95, ISBN 1201844710351

"The smudged / floor glistens with silver tracks, / her watered foot prints to and from / the tub where she floats in almond oil / deep in her sarcophagus of light", writes Sue Hubbard of Pierre Bonnard's wife in the first poem of her collection *Ghost Station*. The poem introduces Hubbard's central theme of obsession both by way of the unfortunate Madame Bonnard's compulsions, and through Bonnard's indefatigable desire to portray his wife about her ablutions. The submergence of its female subject, albeit a picturesque submergence, allows Hubbard to enact her own revisionist preoccupations in poems that are profoundly concerned with loss. Frequently, a visual trigger leads to the imagining of lost moments and the lives for which they metonymically stand, as when, contemplating an abandoned railway line, she imagines a clutch of ghostly passengers: "Think of a bent hair-pin lodged for years under a wooden carriage seat / fallen from a stook of auburn hair, / a single collar-stud trapped beneath / the floor that once fastened small intimacies behind a film of beaded glass...".

Given that Hubbard is also an art critic, the visual sensitivity of these poems is, not unexpectedly, acute, but the reconstructive technique she employs is reminiscent of – among others – Eavan Boland, that high-priestess of lost causes (peasant women, ancient Ireland, artists' wives). Like Boland, Hubbard is sometimes in danger of falling back on a kind of sensuous passivity of rhetoric, which merely echoes the passivity she bemoans: "behind the sophistication of coifed curls, / those earstuds of malachite and pearls, / the plaque of carnelian in the dip of her throat / she stares out full of quiet restraint". Also like Boland, the method can lead her to some implausibly ponderous-sounding utterances as when, later in the same poem, she claims:

"I've been carrying around this museum postcard / for days, struggling to hold her olive-black gaze / across two millennia, trying to interpret the hieroglyphs of death's silent grammar." Here the attempt at empathy translates into an exaggerated attitude.

However this represents a rare false note in *Ghost Station*, because what Hubbard does, she does well. The poems seduce with their coolly reflective imagery and there are moments of brilliantly apt description, as when she describes a "fat chunk of American moon" – an image which immediately brings to mind an outsize slice of American apple pie, and succeeds in surprising by a not-so-fine excess. Hubbard's skill is evident, but the limitations of a strongly descriptive aesthetic are also apparent in this collection. The poems' surface exquisiteness is seldom ruffled, even when they deal with harrowing subjects such as the death of a close relative by suicide, and this luxuriance finds an echo in her sometimes *recherché* vocabulary. Words like "foulard", "tilth", "percale", "bisque", "geest", "triturated" seem less to have battled it out in composition and fully earned their place than to have been chosen for the sake of their exotic gorgeousness. This leads arguably to a possible inapt useage in "Nude in Bathtub", where Hubbard describes "body / and water all one in a miasma / of mist, a haze of lavender blue." "Miasma of mist" sounds good, but "miasma" has an exclusively negative connotation which strikes an off-key note in this context.

Hubbard writes mainly in unrhymed free verse stanzas, from which she extracts some variety. There is an enjoyable sense of her awareness of the poem's shape on the page, her acute eye extending this far also. "Digging to Australia" and "Port Hunter" consist of fractured run-on lines, and in these poems, where she most succeeds in breaking up her work's smooth surface, the outcome is a quickening of the rhythmic pulse, a heightening of the poems' linguistic energy. If Hubbard's considerable descriptive skills were tethered to a more involved rhetoric, a drama of enactment in language, the results might be extraordinary.

CAITRIONA O'REILLY

A singular star

Peter Redgrove, *Sheen*, Stride, £10.95, ISBN 1900152878
Full of Star's Dreaming, tributes to Peter Redgrove by fellow poets,
edited Rupert Loydell, Stride, £5.95, ISBN 1900152193

Peter Redgrove, who is paid full and warm tribute by his fellow poets in *Full of Star's Dreaming*, died in 2003. His poetry was wonderfully fluent, photographically vivid, genial, imaginative, and gets you high. His classic status was recognised in the 1970s but the knowledge seems to have faded more recently. *Sheen* is one of his best volumes. Of the authorities I most often consult, neither Prynne nor the late Martin Seymour-Smith admired his work. Seymour-Smith thought he was just a knock-off of T. F. Powys – an error, since both were simply part of a personalised current which spread uncontrollably with the collapse of organised religion, and we could as well cite David Jones, Dylan Thomas, William Golding – or William Blake. The notion of religion as a set of collectively validated myths has, tentatively, been replaced by that of a neurological state, set off by certain triggers. Collective authentication is replaced by optical vividness:

> A singular star
> 　　　　　　fell from heaven – he
> 　　　　　　　　　　bound it hand and foot,
> To nourish the biblical serpent
> 　　　　　that walks upright
> 　　　　　　　　like a sheen or glory,
> The sheen the look of the sound
> 　　　　　of its scales on the ground
> 　　　　　　　　and the look of its hiss:
> This pyrosome, the female firesnake

Sheen is *glory* in the sense of an aureole, a light of the right brightness to dazzle and destabilise the cortex into a state in which meanings arise spontaneously. Here the meaning is about sexuality – the snake is the one in Genesis. Something about temptation, something about being bound. "Pyrosome" means "body of fire", a self-like thing which has organs and is made of fire. In this poem, Revelation, with the great star that falls from heaven, precedes Genesis, and the star is also Lucifer falling, to become the serpent. "Sheen" occurs also in the second poem in the collection, but not after that. The analogies flow without solidifying into a doctrine. We could argue about in what sense they make sense, but they are beautifully framed and sequenced, and that flow of primary visible wonders makes something quite basic and, behind the eyes, content.

Repeated motifs are patches of bright light, flowing water, female sexuality, and magnets – probably used as examples of highly ordered invisible energies:

> The roads are long metallic
>
>   rays of stars,
>
>   the comet is a great
> Frozen lake flying in the sky, vibrating
>
>   reeds, ice-waterfalls and all,
>
>   a lake of frozen pitch flying,
> A salt marsh flying . . .

The use of bright lights here may be as triggers for a state of flow, in Victor Turner's terms, where, raised out of everyday identities, we act at the same speed as we think, and generate meanings all the time. In flow, there are no wrong moves – everything is bright, pictorial, instantaneous, fully formed. I suppose the "pitch" in the quotation above to be a reference to aromatic carbons in the comet, quite like bitumen; Redgrove made fewer mistakes than most poets because he actually had a grasp of how the universe is composed. The bit about the vibrating reeds is impossibly rich, but might make sense if we looked at a comet close-up. It may also be a Neoplatonist trope (from the *Chaldaean Oracles)*; but the comet/lake analogy is a brilliant imagination of the real.

Like his contemporary at Cambridge, Ted Hughes, Redgrove uses animals as animate myths, their bodies as the horizon enclosing experience, where freedom shifts to givenness. Whereas Hughes is besotted with individual fate, excess violence and death, Redgrove is more processual and serene. He is strong in that part of the sensory spectrum which registers multiple and microscopic objects, moved by subtle energies – "Splashes of rain / Like moth-scales shed" – and his images resonate with subtle and microscopic programs inside us. Maybe the irrational does not consist of monsters but of a swarm intelligence, like drops of rain.

In some poetry, the personality works like dogma; every poem revealing personality. It never varies. So you can only write the same three poems over and over again. An impasse. Acquiring a less rigid vision of psychology is the key to writing a more modern poetry. Relatedly, one historic function of religion, which Redgrove does carry out, is consolation. He shows the ego as endlessly self-healing by means of pictorial narrative, a fluid which pours out and repairs damage, something impulsive, archaic, and intact.

ANDREW DUNCAN

Peter Redgrove

TREE

All the chemical deeds
Of a tall beech in the rain;

It is a perfumer's busy factory,
And the perfumer herself, dressed in rain,

A banquet which is a garment,
Green table-cloth glittering with silver service,

An analytical banquet,
Each drop balanced, weighed, considered, delivered,

Immense detail contrived by the total of leaves
Like the glittering works of a watch,

The immense total the reason
For the quality of the product,

The deluge from above pauses
For inspections of its anatomy

Laid out in detail in the tree,
The soul glittering for a while in a green body,

Soul stretched right down into the cellarage,
The root laboratory where the first separations are performed

With the care also responsible for the quality of light
And the tree's active silhouette

And for the complex music of its tower,
Its tone like thin silver chains and a thousand violins,

The silver hiss which is small rapid vortices spun off
Like hares boxing on to the great banks of

Silence created by air rushing over the cliffs.

ORIENTING BY BROTHEL

Screwing like chinamen, taking five
        to smoke a small cigar outside, they set
                the celestial garden-rocks
Singing, those Chinese Orpheuses,
        these rock musicians,
                the mirror shining in itself
As another birth-passage of polished stone
        in any brothel,
                waking after your pang
To see the world reassemble in its round;
        there is porcelain painted
                with a harmonious couple
Coupling and this charged with energy the food;
        if you stay the night
                there is an unfathomable thirst to die
Into each sweetly-misty morning,
        to roll over and enter for ever
                the mists beyond the dreams.
This Inn is *The Big Dipper*, and it is my own –
        I looked, and then she came!
                The Goddess of Immortality
Bearing her basket brimming with roses walks
        across the yin-water;
                the watery oils of abyssal yin
Do not hinder her,
        she enters her residence established here
                which shines with post-coital deepening
When all the surfaces turn to mirrors
        arranged by the entire Orient.

These two poems by Peter Redgrove are among the last he wrote. We will be printing four more in the autumn. They appear by kind permission of Penelope Shuttle.

Red sky at night

Gillian Clarke, *Making the Beds for the Dead*, Carcanet, £6.95, ISBN 1857547373

Gillian Clarke is Wales's most popular contemporary poet. Long a mainstay feature on the GCSE syllabus, her work has seemed more appealing, more mainstream to many readers than that of the late R. S. Thomas, a poet with whom she shares a fascination for isolation and for epiphany through absence. Certainly, as an organic farmer as well, one might suppose her eminently qualified to explore Wales's annus horribilis, the 2001 Foot and Mouth outbreak – an extended sequence on which provides her with the title for this, her seventh collection. Indeed, *Making the Beds for the Dead* takes the rural community as its centre of gravity and its micro-model for the environmental perils facing the world at large. I expected a challenging and charged read, but for the most part this was not what I got.

There's no doubting Clarke's love of the land and its domestic economy, which she explores with characteristic accessibility and an often excellently realised, deceptively simple description, reminiscent of Hughes:

> Sunrise, and the cattle
> come home for milking,
> slowly, heavily picking their way,
> rolling their oiled machinery
>
> all angles and corners,
> old leather toolbags
> of hammers and saws,
> shoulders and shanks.

("Fox")

It's not hard to see why Clarke is beloved of the exam boards. Her work feels like a workshop exposition of sound poetic technique in form, of the pre-scriptive in the descriptive. But often there's just too much playing safe, and many poems here – though accomplished – are made disappointing by their very neatness. Sometimes Clarke's metaphor, too, seems over-familiar ("the peeled skull / of a frog, like the husk of a planet"; "a pyramid of fruit / bumping north / on the Baghdad road, / piled like skulls"). It's tempting to compare her work with that of another (proudly) accessible Welsh poet also on the syllabus, Sheenagh Pugh. Pugh, like Clarke, may be adept at the quiet lyric, but she's an emboldened risk-taker, defiantly capable of confounding the reader's complacency. For my part, I couldn't help but feel that Clarke should be providing us with a few more questions that demand answers – or maybe a few more answers that pose questions.

This is not to dismiss Clarke's frequently admirable strengths. She's at her best when confronting the ambiguities of the eschatological vision that serves as a recurring theme of the collection. In "Flood" she determines

> When all's said
> and done
> if civilisation drowns
> the last colour to go
> will be gold –
> the light on a glass,
> the prow of a gondola,
> the name on a rosewood piano
> as silence engulfs it

Here, Clarke cleverly inverts the rhetoric of the über-poet of the rural community, Robert Frost. If, for him, "nothing gold can stay", for Clarke, any deluge threatening oblivion merely serves to pare down the essence of the world to light – through art and the spirit – and signals the promise of light's inevitable return. And if, for Frost, creation prefigures destruction, for her, the opposite holds true. It is an unfashionably positive and yet fitting close to a collection with a rather high body count – insofar as sheep are concerned, at any rate.

In the final analysis, though, Clarke's standpoint is curiously and resolutely apolitical and uncontroversial. All well and good as far as pastoral idyll is concerned, but how does any poet reconcile such an approach with the realities of foot and mouth – not least bankruptcy, suicide, isolation and cultural division? If the crisis raised for many some brutally realistic questions about the future of agriculture and its dependent communities, Clarke appears not to have been among them. It's certainly surprising that such a humane poet should so often elide the human. *Making the Beds for the Dead* remains nonetheless an elegant and at times rewarding collection, if a little supine for this reader.

KATHRYN GRAY

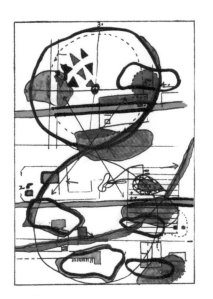

The shiny sounds of crushing lots

Lisa Jarnot, *Ring of Fire*, Salt, £8.95, ISBN 1844710076

> Tell me why you don't
> want to know about the
> snake cults in ancient
> greece and then tell me
> why someone started all
> the tin foil on fire on
> avenue b and then tell
> me the story about osgood
> and ferocious the giant
> squirrels.

("Tell Me Poem")

The first time that I read *Ring of Fire*, I didn't like "Tell Me Poem". It seemed too *faux-naif*: from wide-eyed classicism to comic animals in 9.5 lines. But then I heard Lisa Jarnot read the poem, on CD, in an American monotone between deadpan and deadly serious. And I saw the other thing in it: the tin foil on fire on avenue b.

The image recalls Hopkins on "God's Grandeur" – "like shining from shook foil" – but its oddness is first-hand, a live anarchic fact. Anyone who can bring that into a poem is no naif. The tone of "Tell Me Poem" is, in fact, at least half-sarcastic. Its unanswerable imperatives implicate the reader (who knows "the story") in the substitution of a Looney Tunes sublime for the wonders and terrors of the real world.

Jarnot writes a poetry of high unknowing loaded with known, bathetic things. Her diction is a mixture of the archaic and the contemporary, an unstable register which reflects a widespread dilemma: how to be sincere in a world of cool. "Ye White Antarctic Birds" introduces Romantic polar regions into a rhapsody on New York's art-gallery-lined Upper 57th Street: "you the birds antarctic of the conversations / and the bank machines, you the atm of / longing, the longing for the atm machines".

These poem-sentences throw seemingly immiscible imagery into a syntax of repetition and revision which rolls its ingredients out in fresh connections, disrupted by just-right rhythmic checks and unexpected emotions:

> you the books and phones and atms the bank

machines antarctic, and you the banks and
cabs, and him the one I love, and those who
love me not, and all antarctic longings, and
all the birds and cabs and also on the street
antarctic of this longing.

"And also" is a characteristic phrase of poems that reach after every kind of
thing: "the clicker for / the gas stove [...] and also then Prometheus" ("What
In Fire Did I, Firelover, Starter of Fires, Love?") Their imaginative span is both
thematic and auditory: "the Chinese
in the armies / with the shiny sound
of Johnny Cash", for example, takes
the component sounds of "Chinese"
and spreads them through the next
line. Exotic animals – armadillo,
chinchilla, aardvark – serve as verbal
anchors (zoological referents almost
effaced) for poems which blur the
boundary between a human and
"non-human" world.

This point is made emphati-
cally in the poem "Right View",
where the epithet "human" is
universally applied: a "human
moth", a "human lamp", a "human
mall". Again, the hard fact of that
"mall" (with its "escalator") pays for
the conclusion's Romanticism,
"loving the human, fortunate, / in
all that is alive". In the aftermath of

American Language poetry, Lisa Jarnot returns to the vatic spirit of Black
Mountain, and in particular Robert Duncan, who once wrote: "The
imagination of the cosmos is as immediate to me as the imagination of my
household or my self." Importantly, however, Jarnot has also absorbed the
Language movement's anti-vatic insistence on verbal surface and cultural
detritus. So, in the same poem that declares "I am the empty grain silos of
Bernal Heights and god", she also writes "I can collect cans at all the can and
crushing lots". Jarnot's is a canny kind of naivety.

JEREMY NOEL-TOD

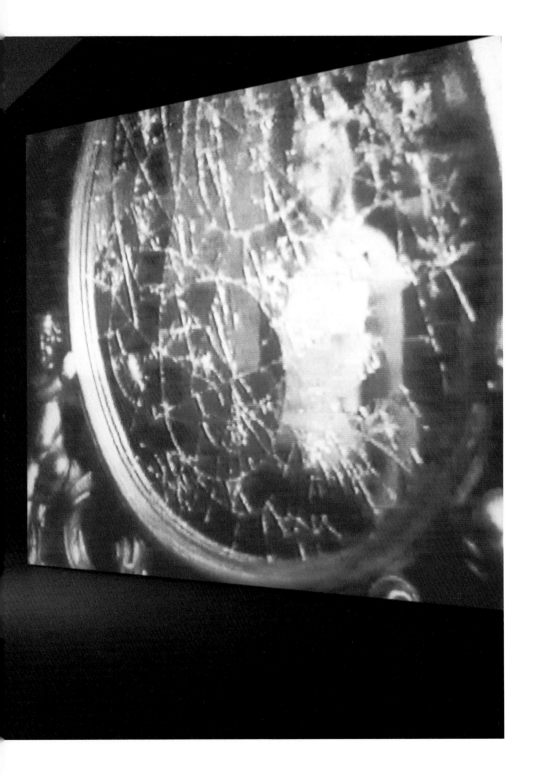

Not taking dictation

Andrew Graham-Yooll and Daniel Samoilovich (editors),
Twenty Poets from Argentina, Redbeck Press, £8.95, ISBN 1904338186

The titles of the poems in this anthology are perhaps indicative: "The Fall", "Mute", "Death Straightforward", "Demolition", "End", "Departure". If you want bright, light verse or celebratory odes, stay clear of modern Argentinian poetry. Not that these are the only titles, but there is little promise of the comfortably concrete in *Twenty Poets From Argentina*, and the governing mood throughout is sombre, sorrowful, reflective.

But there is hope, nonetheless. As Daniel Samoilovich, one of the River Plate's most respected poets and editor of the Buenos Aires periodical *Diario de Poesía*, says in his introduction: "The historical break imposed by the last dictatorship [1976–1983] ... has been overcome". Most of the poets here are under forty and have been marked as children of the generation that was murdered, tortured, "disappeared" and exiled during the Dirty War years. As children, they either witnessed or at least sensed the terror and are affected by this in a variety of ways, political and personal. As Samoilovich suggests, they are also isolated from earlier generations of Argentinian poets through the inevitable historical fracturing such horror imposes on a country's cultural traditions.

Fabián Casas's "Final / End" neatly summarises a social and emotional narrative of four decades: "This is the patio where I was small. / The tiles are worn and the plants / have grown in the cracks in the wall", he begins. You might think for an instant you were still in the romantic refuge that Borges made of his myopically mythologised "eternal" Buenos Aires. But Casas wraps up his poem with a vision of a city where couples no longer kiss on park benches (as they do, for hours, on the leafy plazas of Buenos Aires) and "the only vestige of love / will be / porn videos".

Somewhere between these extremes of nostalgia and resignation all these poets find a voice. Washington Cucurto, one of the few non-white writers represented, tackles mortality with an exuberant tropical irony, one foot in a twenty-first century slum, the other in a pre-Columbian legend. Martín Prieto, Alejandro Rubio and Laura Wittner seem to be trapped in a patio / café / garden / seaside resort with only memory (or the idea of memory), longing and melancholy – those famed Argentinian modes – for company. But in Prieto's wish to have his old job back and a pastel-shaded life, and in Wittner's hazy childhood scenes, there is more than the sadness of recollection. Death and darkness seem always to be at the edge of imagining. As Carolina Cazes advises, in her powerful inventory of a demolished squat: "sometimes one searches / without knowing what to search for / and one gets, / if one gets, / what is not / wanted".

Martin Gambarotta's poems are more self-consciously abstract studies – they read like notes towards a poem and leave something like the kind of impression which art-house horror films or files of photographic evidence leave. He owes a debt to T. S. Eliot, Julio Cortázar and also Alejandra Pizarnik, the latter an unknown in Britain but of seminal importance to Argentinian poetry since the 1970s.

Taken as a whole, the collection is rarely an easy read, but this is searching, committed verse in a society where (since the severing of the radical idealisms of Guevarista militancy) both language and memory have, like human bodies, been tortured. Poetry provides an opportunity for precision and, perhaps above all, for a considered analysis of human and societal relations that is free of facile sentiment and bogus intensity. This is essentially educated poetry of the big city, yet most of the authors strive to slow down thought, the poets distancing themselves from the maelstroms of mediated language and the frantic rhythms of urban survival.

Samoilovich summarises the main tradition that precedes this latest school, highlighting the richness and variety of his younger colleagues' work. He praises the ethos – or ethic – of "visibility" that guides their writing. In all forty-odd poems, there is an impassioned will to rend illusory surfaces and shun false gods. Calmly, incisively, Argentinian poetry is moving forward.

Anglo-Argentinian author and journalist Andrew Graham-Yooll, himself an accomplished poet of the previous generation, handles the texts (presented here in parallel form) with an ear attuned to the syntax and sensibilities of River Plate castellano, without eschewing the musical requirements of the English.

CHRIS MOSS

Poet in the Gallery

MARK FORD

Edward Hopper
27 May – 5 September 2004
Tate Modern

Edward Hopper was not much given to making statements about the evolution or meanings of his paintings. "If you could say it in words", he pointed out to a reporter from *Time* magazine in 1956, "there'd be no need to paint." Famously taciturn, he left it to his garrulous wife, Jo, who was also a painter, although not a very successful one, to do battle with art critics and journalists. Occasionally, however, he'd offer up an Emersonian nugget of wisdom or defiance: "The only real influence I've ever had", runs my favourite of these, "was myself."

Hopper was a voracious reader of Emerson, and the iconic status of pictures such as "House by the Railroad" or "Nighthawks" derives in part from the way they evoke American traditions of what Emerson called self-reliance. The isolated, shuttered house, cut off from the viewer by the railroad tracks and surrounded by a remorselessly blank sky, and the noir-ish couple in the all-night diner, each buried in incommunicable thought, have become globally recognized signifiers of Americanness; like so many of Hopper's pictures, they hang equivocally suspended between freedom and inertia, glamour and banality, some obscure sense of will or purpose and hopeless emptiness.

Hopper's work has been so mediated through poster reproductions and the uses made of it by film directors such as Alfred Hitchcock (whose design for the sinister mansion of Norman Bates in *Psycho* was based on "House by the Railroad"), David Lynch, Douglas Sirk, and Terence Malick, that it's hard to disentangle his images from some generalized concept of "the American Imagination". There is even a book called *Edward Hopper and the American Imagination*, edited by Deborah Lyons, which reproduces stories and poems by such as Paul Auster, Norman Mailer, William Kennedy and Galway Kinnell that contain no references at all to Hopper, but are claimed somehow to reflect his "vision".

It is claimed in the introduction to this volume that "Hopper shares with the American writers who were his contemporaries a commitment to speak a plain language". How unplain, however, and how uncommitted, is the first picture in this exhibition, painted between 1902 and 1904 while Hopper was a

student at the New York School of Art: measuring nine by twelve inches and painted in oil on board, it depicts the back of a figure, probably a woman, reading in the front row of a deserted theatre. The stage, which occupies the top half of the picture, is a greyish murk. Only the proscenium arch stands out clearly from the sepulchral gloom, the first of many frames and thresholds, of windows opening onto other worlds, that seem to promise some kind of meaning, but never deliver it. Hopper's final picture, "Two Comedians" (1966), is also set in the theatre. This time, however, the stage is lighted and flanked by artificial greenery, and a man and woman, recognizably Hopper and his wife, dressed in pierrot-costume, take a final bow. "That's all folks!", they seem to be saying.

Like earlier rugged American individualists such as Benjamin Franklin, or James Fenimore Cooper, or his great hero, Thomas Eakins, Edward Hopper developed his distinctively American take on the American scene by going to Paris. There, he fell under the spell of Courbet, Degas, and Manet, and painted some exquisite empty interiors and deserted courtyards. His return to America seems to have both shocked and stalled him: "It seemed awfully crude and raw here when I got back", he later commented; "It took me ten years to get over Europe." He spent a miserable decade and a half working as a freelance commercial illustrator, and wasn't offered a commercial solo gallery show until 1924, when he was forty-two. On the other hand, only six years later "House by the Railroad" was the first painting to enter the Museum of Modern Art's permanent collection, and the following year the Whitney paid $3,000 for "Early Sunday Morning", and the Metropolitan $4,500 for "Tables for Ladies". Hopper has never really been out of fashion since. He not only withstood the onslaught of Abstract Expressionism, but won praise from leading exponents such as Mark Rothko and Willem de Kooning, while in the mid-sixties his work was even hailed as a vital precursor and catalyst for Pop Art.

It's not hard to guess Hopper's private response to such tributes. "You kill me!" he muttered when his friend Lloyd Goodrich informed him he had just given a lecture comparing a Hopper painting with one by Mondrian. The equation he felt his art, and the art he valued, set itself was best expressed by a quotation from Goethe that he carried around in his wallet:

> The beginning and the end of all [artistic] activity is the reproduction of the
> world that surrounds me by means of the world that is in me, all things being
> grasped, related, re-created, moulded and reconstructed in a personal form and
> an original manner.

He came up with a more succinct version of this theory when pressed to explain what he was striving for in the magnificent late painting, "Sun in an Empty Room": "I'm after me."

The "me" Hopper's paintings embody is least evident in his stylised, often rather clunky figures. It's as if they know they're acting, and self-consciousness has rendered them rigid. The paintings' expansive inner dramas are played out, instead, by competing rectangles or rhomboids of light, by the interplay of wall and window, by shadows streaking an empty sidewalk, by red and blue drapes in the brightly-lit window of a drugstore at night, by the mute pathos of suitcases, telephones, lamps and decanters. The narratives his scenarios at first seem to illustrate never materialize: the urge to decode the situation which first hooks the viewer soon gives way to a relaxed, spacious awareness of the invitation his pictures offer to enjoy melancholy on its own terms.

And though the protagonists themselves are nearly always deep in reverie, we are not encouraged to identify with them or probe their thoughts. Our reveries must not be confused with theirs, for that would be to contravene one of the central laws of self-reliance: "To believe your own thought," wrote Emerson, "to believe that what is true for you in your private thought is true for all men – that is genius. Speak your latent conviction, and it shall be the universal sense." Hopper believed, and in a review quoted, this dictum, but he didn't find it easy to follow. In his agonizing struggle to paint, to find outer scenes he could transform into expressions of his "private thought", he evolved a pictorial language that so insistently draws attention to its own framing techniques and artifices that it's baffling to think he was often called both a realist and a regionalist.

A life-long devotee of stage and screen, Hopper's most complex effects depend on the highly original ways in which his paintings formulate the thrills and anxieties of spectatorship. His pictures seem disquieting not because they convincingly illustrate alienation or loneliness or the modern condition, but because they are so singularly incurious about the characters who inhabit them. The men all come from central casting, and the women are invariably versions of his wife, who modelled for nearly all of Hopper's female figures, even, in her sixties, dressing up in tight skirt and high heels to play the curvaceous young secretary in "Office at Night". The potential corniness of Hopper's scenes is defused, in his best work, by the way the setting neutralises our interest in whatever is preoccupying the leads. The preliminary sketches for "Office at Night", for instance, reveal him experimenting with different angles of vision, and deciding in the end on a kind of semi-crane shot that empties out the narrative potential of the scene. As in nineteenth-century American painting more explicitly concerned with the sublime, the epic canvases of such as Cole or Church or Bierstadt, it is the people who look out of place. "Maybe I'm not very human", Hopper once mused; "What I wanted to do was paint sunlight on the side of the house."

This retrospective features a fair percentage of "classic" Hoppers, though not my favourite, the "New York Movie" of 1939. A couple of the mid-to-late pictures included here, such as "Summertime" (1943) or "Morning Sun" (1952), seem to me pretty much ruined by the awkwardness of the central figure, and it's the pre-Second World War and very late works that I found most enchanting. His best work really does cast an odd, wholly distinctive spell; for about a week after seeing this show I found myself peering into lighted rooms at night, brooding on office furniture, watching the way the sun moved across wall and living room floor. The Hopper effect has been well characterised by the American poet John Hollander in a lyric inspired by "Sun in an Empty Room". "We may finally say", the poem concludes,

> that, like the painter,
> It was ourselves that we were after,
> Filled with the minding of the light that dwells
> In the inexhaustible flatness of painted
> Room, of what we stand before.

Artist's Notes

Susan Hiller was born in Tallahassee, Florida in 1940 but has lived and worked in the UK for most of her eminent artistic career. She has had numerous highly prestigious exhibitions, and currently her work is enjoying a major showing at Baltic, Centre for Contemporary Art, Newcastle Upon Tyne, in the exhibition "Recall" (selected by James Lingwood of ArtAngel). The selection of images here aims to profile some of the concerns that are dealt with in Hiller's many installations, Internet works, sculptures and writings.

"Wild Talents" (1997) consists of two large projections, made up from film and television footage that explores the uncontrollable psychic powers associated with children, such as telekinesis. Against this backdrop, objects and lights are displayed that represent different religious communities. This work explores popular fears and misconceptions, and Hiller encourages the viewer to interrogate the nature of faith and the way we interpret belief.

For "Dream Mapping", Hiller invited 10 participants to develop a graphic system for recording their dreams. To achieve this they all slept in a field for three days in the Hampshire countryside in an area famous for the number of "fairy rings" or circles. There is a myth that if you step into a fairy-ring, you enter fairy-land. Using a pre-defined system, every morning the participants recorded their dreams on special pads. They then noted similarities between the different dreams and made collective dream maps, one of which is illustrated here alongside an image of a group of the participants. These works were formally presented in 1986 at the ICA in London.

Susan Hiller appears courtesy of Timothy Taylor gallery with thanks to Timothy Taylor and Faye Fleming.

FRED MANN

❧

Poetry Review would like to thank Fred Mann for the excellence and generosity with which he has curated the art pages of the magazine over the past year.

Letter to the Editors

It's good to see Pauline Stainer getting some attention. She is a marvellous poet and we should hear a good deal more of her work. Several of Andrew Duncan's statements in his review of *The Lady and the Hare* hit the point memorably, such as Stainer's "gathering objects of veneration, and forms of words to hymn them, in one".

I can offer two points of detail, which may be helpful. As Duncan says, referring to the poem "The Ice-pilot Speaks", "Baldur was shot with weapons-grade mistletoe by a blind god". It might be worth sketching out the mythical background to this. Baldur's parents, Odin and Frigga, sought protection of their son by prevailing upon all living creatures, plants, metals and stones to vow solemnly not to harm him. The only thing to which this entreaty was not made was the mistletoe growing upon an oak because it was considered inoffensive. However, dirty old Loki, the god of fire, was jealous of Baldur and heard about the protection afforded him. He made arrow shafts from the mistletoe and arranged for Hodur, the blind god, to shoot Baldur. You can guess the rest. Duncan is interesting on sources and I am grateful for the references to G. Wilson Knight. I suggest also that the old favourite *Myths of the Norsemen* by H. A. Guerber (1909 but now reprinted) may be a source.

Duncan queries the title, *The Lady and the Hare*. It is taken from the title of a poem in the volume (p.77). The hounds in the chase freeze at the Lady's calm and "sensed in the cold apse / of her breast / both the dove and the bone" but "Today we started no hare . . ." Duncan conjectures that the hare may be a hieroglyph, and this could be true, for hieroglyphs, escutcheons and emblems have a consistent presence in Stainer's poetry. But Duncan also mentions the hare as a female symbol as "picked up in David Harsent's recent collection, *Marriage*". This is also true, but there is more to the hare than that.

Brewer's Dictionary, under the entry for "Hare", states: "it is unlucky for a hare to cross your path, because witches were said to transform themselves into hares. ... According to mediaeval 'science', the hare was a most melancholy beast, and ate wild succory in the hope of curing itself". My copy of *Brewer's* is 1920s, so the modern edition may not contain the reference.

Thanks for *Poetry Review*, Spring 2004. I'm especially grateful to have the selection of readings from 2003 *Into Words Poetry* on CD.

Alex Smith

The *Poetry Review* Crossword No. 4

The sender of the first correct solution opened on 1 September receives a cash prize of £20. Entries should be addressed to *Poetry Review* Crossword, 22 Betterton Street, London WC2H 9BX.

set by ANDRONYMOUS

Across

9 Poet graduates halfway home (5)
10 No longer do notes, just the right coins (5,4)
11 Duplicates court-martial's corrupt lack of tort (9)
12 Who sang the first, much meandering, hero (5)
13 Writer makes filthier sounds after topless writer returns (6)
14 Alliterative poet redrafted Lucy around new foot (8)
17 Medieval poet's work: after National Insurance, a wage goes back into the wallet, ultimately (3,6,4)
21 Rust can develop after initial exposure to Old Italian (8)
23 Fizzy pop has left only fragments (6)
25 MOR writer? (5)
27 Venetian ruler takes in Lewis and Gardner's "Man of Bronze" (3,6)
28 Conflict with tiny weapons? (6,3)
29 Bring together points, separated by an operculum (5)

Down

1 Turn to sin, but turn elegiac (3, 4)
2 "Is the advert back to front?" hazards the identical twin (8)
3 Swamps in which one preceded, for example, one's breakfast, in one's cups (6,4)
4 Score after 5's plant (5)
5 Typical artist, vaguely pickled (9)
6 It can help to start with a feeling of irritation (4)
7 Repeat of genteel morning repulses insurgents (3-3)
8 Make stone dog, perhaps, if in empty residency (7)
15 Seaside streets somehow suit élan (10)
16 4's sum is 5, deducing badly (3,3,3)
18 Stress of wide space and acidity in the same state (8)
19 Camp David, not keen on French water and farcical chap (7)
20 Put down cow, for example, and save last penny (7)
22 Welsh hero (who was Scottish) (6)
24 A cereal crop becomes a mighty tree (5)
26 Let's begin after I've given up sin (4)

Editorial
Government and the Value of Poetry

A document which promises to influence British poetry emerged recently from an unlikely source. In May of this year Tessa Jowell, Secretary of State for Culture, published an essay entitled "Government and the Value of Culture". Ordinarily such a statement would drop happily below the radar; Secretaries of State for Culture are marginal figures in government, and what they have to say about "the arts" is typically only of interest to bureaucrats. Jowell's essay, as has been widely acknowledged already, is significantly different from most such pronouncements; at least in the clarity and purposefulness of its thinking.

Jowell opens her essay with reference to Beveridge's five giants of poverty – want, disease, ignorance, squalor, and idleness. Jowell identifies a sixth giant, "the poverty of aspiration". "Engagement with culture," she argues, "can help alleviate this poverty of aspiration." "The poverty of aspiration" is a thrilling prhase from a government minister, especially for anybody who has experienced, in whatever role, the mediocrity which currently informs the state education system's sense of culture, and the intellectual and cultural dis-enfranchisement which that can produce. But then Jowell is hardly the first minister involved with culture to call for the arts to perform a kind of outreach. Where her essay differs is in its sense of the kind and quality of art which should be reaching out. Dismissing the term "high culture" as a useless remnant of an old debate, Jowell instead makes a distinction between "simplicity and complexity, between entertainment on the one hand and cultural engagement on the other". It is the latter element of "culture" Jowell singles out for attention, and important statements follow:

> Complex cultural activity is not just a pleasurable hinterland for the public, a fall back after the important things – work and paying tax – are done. It is at the heart of what it means to be a fully developed human being. Government should be concerned that so few aspire to it, and has a responsibility to do what it reasonably can to raise the quantity and quality of that aspiration.

Furthermore, Jowell argues, "The reluctance of so many to attempt that challenge [of grappling with complex cultural work] is a terrible waste of human potential, with a concomitant loss of human realisation." The word here, it should be noticed, is not "difficulty" – as if being "difficult" were either a good thing, or a bad thing, in itself – but "complexity". Art, whatever else it does, has recourse to complex, and complexes of, thought. There is, Jowell asserts, a releasing of human potential when people are permitted to engage with the fullness of art. Art makes humans more human.

Or rather, some art does. Reversing a trend in public thinking about the arts which has damaged culture for at least two decades, Jowell dismisses the idea of "accessibility". The issue is not, as she sees plainly, that art should be accessible, but that all people should have "access" to art:

> So in seeking access, we want to make sure we are supplying access to the best. Access to the substandard is access to disappointment which will translate into an unwillingness to keep paying. It will not inspire or raise levels of aspiration, and in the end it is not worthwhile. That is why excellence has to be kept at the heart of cultural subsidy, and that is what we must insist on.

Jowell's example of best practice is Otto Klemperer, who as director of the Kroll Opera in Weimar Berlin had the task of making "high quality opera available to working class subscribers . . . . The experiment showed that access and excellence could co-exist. It was shut down by the Nazis."

"Government and the Value of Culture" articulates a properly democratic vision of how art benefits citizens because it does not imply that citizens deserve second best. Still, there are two aspects of the essay that concern *Poetry Review*. The first, baldly, is that while it mentions fine art, music and dance as instances of cultural activity, it at no point names poetry. The second is that, while long on aspiration, it is short on the practicality of *generating* aspiration – though, in fairness to Jowell, the essay is clearly marked "for discussion".

From *Poetry Review's* point of view, what is at issue here is joined-up government. Jowell's essay has to do with arts funding, and it is good to think that, in future, funding for poetry initiatives will be linked to "access to excellence" not "accessibility". In particular, Jowell is at pains to insist that arts funding should no longer be predicated on the meeting of targets; targets, as every public and voluntary sector worker knows, being New Labour's particular funding fetish. Even so, it remains the case that, where poetry is concerned, most people's form of access is through education, and the practice of education, more than most public practices in the past seven years, has been corrupted by the meeting of targets, from SATs to the RAE. It is not so easy, in other words, for the Secretary of State for Culture to slay the poverty of aspiration when the Secretary of State for Education is impoverishing the experience of learning.

These reservations notwithstanding, *Poetry Review* applauds Tessa Jowell's statement, and is delighted at her suggestion that it should be the beginning of a debate. The web address at which the document can be consulted is **www.culture.gov.uk/global/publications/archive_2004/ Government_Value_of_Culture.htm.** Letters to the editors please.